Exploring English Short Stories

Oksun Kang · Steven Reeder

Shinasa

본 저서는 2009년도 동서대학교 학술연구비 지원으로 제작되었습니다.

Contents

MP3 files can be downloaded at publisher's homepage : www.shinasa.co.kr

MP3 files can be downloaded at publisher's homepage : www.shinasa.co.kr

Preface

Short stories are a dying art form. Few artists write them because fewer people are reading them. The market is not what it used to be. In fact, movies have all but replaced short stories. Movies, having to be short themselves, are nothing more than short stories on screen. Short stories, like movies, usually follow a single point of view and have time or space to pursue a single major plotline with only a few well fleshed out central characters. Such structure gives the movies accessibility. It also makes short stories a wonderful window to the world that can be glanced upon in just one reading session. Reading short stories allows us to go deeper into the story than a novel and to savor the techniques the writer uses to draw a picture in our mind. Short stories are like movies, except we control the visuals. How sad it is losing popularity.

The very artistic nature of short stories also makes them more difficult to read. The language is often more poetic and the choice of words more deliberate. This can make it difficult for a student whose second language is English. An exercise in literary appreciation can turn into frustration. Enter *Exploring English Short Stories*. The purpose of this book is rather simple: to introduce second language learners to the wonderful prose of short stories. To make these stories more accessible, we have introduced the authors with a brief biography that can help students understand the environment and situations in which they were written. After reading the story, I have included an analysis to help the student understand one of the many different ways of analyzing a story. Since all of these stories were written

Introduction of the Author

O. Henry (1862-1910)

William Sydney Porter, better known by his pen name O. Henry, lived a life as exciting as the fiction he wrote. He was born in Greensboro, North Carolina where his great uncle served as governor. After his mother died of tuberculosis when he was three, he and his father moved in with his grandmother. He later lived with his aunt and attended her elementary school. Though he loved to read and his aunt continued to tutor him, he quit school by the age of fifteen and started working as a clerk in his uncle's pharmacy and then received an apprenticeship as a pharmacist. At the age of twenty, Porter moved to southern Texas to alleviate a chronic cough condition he had contracted. He worked on a sheep ranch for two years and eloped with Athol Estes, a seventeen year old who also had tuberculosis. His son died at birth, and he had a daughter a year later. His health improved, so he moved to Austin, Texas where he found work as a clerk in a real-estate office. He also worked as a pharmacist, draftsman, and a bank teller for the First National Bank. Interestingly enough, though the pastoral life had cured his illnesses, the stress and demands of urban living probably drew him to drinking heavily, 2.3 liters of whiskey a day, which would have a detrimental effect on his health later in life.

Porter moved to Houston, Texas in 1896 to write columns for the Post. A year later, the First National Bank was audited and Porter's poor book keeping got him in trouble. He was arrested for embezzlement, a crime he denied committing, and was transferred back to Austin to stand trial. After his father-in-law bailed him out of jail, he fled to New Orleans, Louisiana and then to Honduras, Central America. Since his wife was sick and dying, she could not meet him in Central America, so he returned to America to face the courts. Athol soon died of tuberculosis. A little less than a year later, Porter was also found guilty of embezzlement and sentenced to five years at the Ohio penitentiary in 1898, whereupon he was released in three years for good behavior. Though Porter had written several stories before his imprisonment, he penned fourteen short stories while incarcerated, all under various pen names, to help support his daughter. After his release from prison he changed his name to O. Henry. Many speculations arise as to why he settled on such a name. One is from Porter himself, who said he chose "Henry" randomly from a newspaper and then settled on an easy initial to write, "O." He gave other reasons in other interviews, causing others to speculate on the origins as well. American writers and intellectuals even surmised that the name O. Henry originated from the name of his prison, **Oh**io p**en**itentia**ry**. Other speculators say that the name came from the prison warden Orren Henry.

By 1902, Porter had moved to New York, where many of his stories were to take place, to fully concentrate on his writing. One of his last anthology collections *The Four Million* (1906) expressed his appreciations for his readers, especially the people of New York—New York had a population of four million at the time of publication. Most noteworthy of this publication was the short story "The Gift of the Magi," which, next to Charles Dickens' *A Christmas Carol*, is the most adapted Christmas story. Porter became a prolific writer like Guy de Maupassant, and wrote a story a week over a three year period. During the last eight years of his life, he published 381 stories under the O. Henry pseudonym. Most of his stories were collected in anthologies (ten in all) and his grand total of stories written stands over 600. As can be assumed, not every story he wrote was a classic, but his ironic wit and twist endings endeared him to a wide following of readers, while most literary critics ignored him. Having such an extensive experience from living in both rural and urban settings, visiting foreign countries, and spending time in a jail, Porter drew upon these to depict all the different aspects of American life in his time. Most of his stories are masterfully crafted; just about any short story anthology includes an O. Henry staple story. Thus, he had become one of the most popular American writers.

Porter's heavy drinking had so affected his health that by 1908 his condition had worsened, interfering with his ability to write. On June 5, 1910, William Sydney Porter died from a liver disease and an enlarged heart.

The Gift of the Magi

One dollar and eighty-seven cents[1]. That was all. And sixty cents[2] of it was in pennies. Pennies saved one and two at a time by bulldozing the grocer and the vegetable man and the butcher until one's cheeks burned with the silent imputation of parsimony[3] that such close dealing implied. Three times Della counted it. One dollar and eighty-seven cents. And the next day would be Christmas.

There was clearly nothing to do but flop down on the shabby little couch and howl. So Della did it. Which instigates the moral reflection that life is made up of sobs, sniffles, and smiles, with sniffles predominating.

While the mistress of the home is gradually subsiding from the first stage to the second, take a look at the home. A furnished flat at $8 per week.[4] It did not exactly beggar description,[5] but it certainly had that word on the lookout for the men-

1. **one dollar and eighty-seven cents ($1.87)**: inflation adjusted to be about $41.00 (please note that the inflation conversion is to give a sense of how much said amount would be in today's American market. It does not indicate exact value or buying power)
2. **sixty cents**: inflation adjusted to be about $14.00 (similar to saying that 14 dollars was in single bills)
3. **imputation of parsimony**: accusing someone of being stingy
4. **$8** : inflation adjusted to about $177.00
5. **beggar description...mendicancy squad**: a play on words where "beggar" here means inadequate, in that the apartment the Young's live in did not seem that inadequate (beggar) but beggars (mendicancy squad) would feel at home living in it. This seems to say that the value they had to pay did not equal the run-down state of the apartment

dicancy squad.[6]

In the vestibule below was a letter-box into which no letter would go, and an electric button from which no mortal finger could coax a ring. Also appertaining thereunto was a card bearing the name "Mr. James Dillingham Young."

The "Dillingham" had been flung to the breeze during a former period of prosperity when its possessor was being paid $30 per week.[7] Now, when the income was shrunk to $20,[8] the letters of "Dillingham" looked blurred, as though they were thinking seriously of contracting to a modest and unassuming D. But whenever Mr. James Dillingham Young came home and reached his flat above he was called "Jim" and greatly hugged by Mrs. James Dillingham Young, already introduced to you as Della. Which is all very good.

Della finished her cry and attended to her cheeks with the powder rag. She stood by the window and looked out dully at a grey cat walking a grey fence in a grey backyard. Tomorrow would be Christmas Day, and she had only $1.87 with which to buy Jim a present. She had been saving every penny she could for months, with this result. Twenty dollars a week doesn't go far. Expenses had been greater than she had calculated. They always are. Only $1.87 to buy a present for Jim. Her Jim. Many a happy hour she had spent planning for something nice for him. Something fine and rare and sterling[9] — something just a little bit near to being worthy of the honor of being owned by Jim.

6. **mendicancy squad** : beggars
7. **$30** : inflation adjusted to about $664.00
8. **$20** : inflation adjusted to about $443.00
9. **sterling**: fine silver

There was a pier-glass[10] between the windows of the room. Perhaps you have seen a pier-glass in an $8 flat.[11] A very thin and very agile person may, by observing his reflection in a rapid sequence of longitudinal strips, obtain a fairly accurate conception of his looks. Della, being slender, had mastered the art.

Suddenly she whirled from the window and stood before the glass. Her eyes were shining brilliantly, but her face had lost its color within twenty seconds. Rapidly she pulled down her hair and let it fall to its full length.

Now, there were two possessions of the James Dillingham Youngs in which they both took a mighty pride. One was Jim's gold watch that had been his father's and his grandfather's. The other was Della's hair. Had the Queen of Sheba[12] lived in the flat across the airshaft, Della would have let her hair hang out the window some day to dry just to depreciate Her Majesty's jewels and gifts. Had King Solomon[13] been the janitor, with all his treasures piled up in the basement, Jim would have pulled out his watch every time he passed, just to see him pluck at his beard from envy.

So now Della's beautiful hair fell about her, rippling and shining like a cascade of brown waters. It reached below her knee and made itself almost a garment for her. And then she did it up again nervously and quickly. Once she faltered for a minute and stood still while a tear or two splashed on the worn red carpet.

10. **pier-glass**: a long mirror through which to view your whole body
11. **flat**: apartment
12. **Queen of Sheba**: legendary queen mentioned in the Bible who ruled an area now in modern Ethiopia; famous for showering Solomon with caravans of riches after he solved her riddle
13. **King Solomon**: legendary ruler of Israel mentioned in the Bible; famous for his wealth and wisdom

On went her old brown jacket; on went her old brown hat. With a whirl of skirts and with the brilliant sparkle still in her eyes, she fluttered out the door and down the stairs to the street.

Where she stopped the sign read: "Mme. Sofronie. Hair Goods of All Kinds." One flight up Della ran, and collected herself, panting. Madame, large, too white, chilly, hardly looked the "Sofronie."

"Will you buy my hair?" asked Della.

"I buy hair," said Madame. "Take yer[14] hat off and let's have a sight at the looks of it."

Down rippled the brown cascade. "Twenty dollars," said Madame, lifting the mass with a practiced hand.

"Give it to me quick," said Della.

Oh, and the next two hours tripped by on rosy wings. Forget the hashed[15] metaphor. She was ransacking the stores for Jim's present.

She found it at last. It surely had been made for Jim and no one else. There was no other like it in any of the stores, and she had turned all of them inside out. It was a platinum fob chai n[16] simple and chaste in design, properly proclaiming its value by substance alone and not by meretricious[17] ornamentation—as all good things should do. It was even worthy of The Watch. As soon as she saw it she knew that it must be Jim's. It was like him. Quietness and value—the description applied to both.

---

14. **yer**: colloquial for "your"
15. **hashed**: messy
16. **fob chain**: a chain that is attached to a pocket watched and then secured to a fob (the small pocket attached to the inside of the front pocket on a pair of pants)
17. **meretricious**: flashy; overly ornamental

Twenty-one dollars[18] they took from her for it, and she hurried home with the 87 cents.[19] With that chain on his watch Jim might be properly anxious about the time in any company. Grand as the watch was, he sometimes looked at it on the sly on account of the old leather strap that he used in place of a chain.

When Della reached home her intoxication[20] gave way a little to prudence and reason. She got out her curling irons and lighted the gas and went to work repairing the ravages made by generosity added to love. Which is always a tremendous task, dear friends—a mammoth task.

Within forty minutes her head was covered with tiny, close-lying curls that made her look wonderfully like a truant[21] schoolboy. She looked at her reflection in the mirror long, carefully, and critically.

"If Jim doesn't kill me," she said to herself, "before he takes a second look at me, he'll say I look like a Coney Island[22] chorus girl. But what could I do—oh! what could I do with a dollar and eighty-seven cents?"

At 7 o'clock the coffee was made and the frying-pan was on the back of the stove hot and ready to cook the chops.[23]

Jim was never late. Della doubled the fob chain in her hand and sat on the corner of the table near the door that he always entered. Then she heard his step on the stair away down on the first flight, and she turned white for just a moment. She had a

18. **twenty-one dollars**: inflation adjusted to about $465.00

19. **87 cents**: inflation adjusted to about $19.00

20. **intoxication**: excitement

21 **truant**: absent from school without permission

22. **Coney Island**: a famous resort district in New York where gambling and prostitution abounded; less reputable than it is today

23. **chops**: pork chops; a type of steak that is made from pork

habit for saying little silent prayers about the simplest everyday things, and now she whispered: "Please God, make him think I am still pretty."

The door opened and Jim stepped in and closed it. He looked thin and very serious. Poor fellow, he was only twenty-two—and to be burdened with a family! He needed a new overcoat and he was without gloves.

Jim stopped inside the door, as immovable as a setter[24] at the scent of quail. His eyes were fixed upon Della, and there was an expression in them that she could not read, and it terrified her. It was not anger, nor surprise, nor disapproval, nor horror, nor any of the sentiments that she had been prepared for. He simply stared at her fixedly with that peculiar expression on his face.

Della wriggled off the table and went for him.

"Jim, darling," she cried, "don't look at me that way. I had my hair cut off and sold because I couldn't have lived through Christmas without giving you a present. It'll grow out again—you won't mind, will you? I just had to do it. My hair grows awfully fast. Say 'Merry Christmas!' Jim, and let's be happy. You don't know what a nice—what a beautiful, nice gift I've got for you."

"You've cut off your hair?" asked Jim, laboriously, as if he had not arrived at that patent[25] fact yet even after the hardest mental labor.

"Cut it off and sold it," said Della. "Don't you like me just as well, anyhow? I'm me without my hair, ain't[26] I?"

24. **setter**: a hunting dog
25. **patent**: obvious
26. **ain't**: colloquial contraction for "am I not"

Jim looked about the room curiously.

"You say your hair is gone?" he said, with an air almost of idiocy.

"You needn't look for it," said Della. "It's sold, I tell you—sold and gone, too. It's Christmas Eve, boy. Be good to me, for it went for you. Maybe the hairs of my head were numbered," she went on with sudden serious sweetness, "but nobody could ever count my love for you. Shall I put the chops on, Jim?"

Out of his trance Jim seemed quickly to wake. He enfolded his Della. For ten seconds let us regard with discreet scrutiny some inconsequential object in the other direction. Eight dollars a week or a million a year—what is the difference? A mathematician or a wit would give you the wrong answer. The magi[27] brought valuable gifts, but that was not among them. This dark assertion will be illuminated later on.

Jim drew a package from his overcoat pocket and threw it upon the table.

"Don't make any mistake, Dell," he said, "about me. I don't think there's anything in the way of a haircut or a shave or a shampoo that could make me like my girl any less. But if you'll unwrap that package you may see why you had me going a while at first."

White fingers and nimble tore at the string and paper. And then an ecstatic scream of joy; and then, alas! a quick feminine change to hysterical tears and wails, necessitating the immediate employment of all the comforting powers of the lord of the flat.

For there lay The Combs—the set of combs, side and back, that Della had worshipped long in a Broadway[28] window.

---

27. **magi**: in the Bible, the three wise men who brought the infant Jesus expensive gifts as homage

Beautiful combs, pure tortoise shell, with jeweled rims—just the shade to wear in the beautiful vanished hair. They were expensive combs, she knew, and her heart had simply craved and yearned over them without the least hope of possession. And now, they were hers, but the tresses[29] that should have adorned the coveted adornments were gone.

But she hugged them to her bosom, and at length she was able to look up with dim eyes and a smile and say: "My hair grows so fast, Jim!"

And them Della leaped up like a little singed cat and cried, "Oh, oh!"

Jim had not yet seen his beautiful present. She held it out to him eagerly upon her open palm. The dull precious metal seemed to flash with a reflection of her bright and ardent[30] spirit.

"Isn't it a dandy, Jim? I hunted all over town to find it. You'll have to look at the time a hundred times a day now. Give me your watch. I want to see how it looks on it."

Instead of obeying, Jim tumbled down on the couch and put his hands under the back of his head and smiled.

"Dell," said he, "let's put our Christmas presents away and keep 'em[31] a while. They're too nice to use just at present. I sold the watch to get the money to buy your combs. And now suppose you put the chops on."

The magi, as you know, were wise men—wonderfully wise men—who brought gifts to the Babe in the manger. They invented the art of giving Christmas presents. Being wise, their

28. **Broadway**: a wide avenue in Manhattan, New York; famous for theaters.
29. **tress**: locks of curly hair
30. **ardent**: passionate
31. **'em**: colloquial for "them"

gifts were no doubt wise ones, possibly bearing the privilege of exchange in case of duplication. And here I have lamely related to you the uneventful chronicle of two foolish children in a flat who most unwisely sacrificed for each other the greatest treasures of their house. But in a last word to the wise of these days let it be said that of all who give gifts these two were the wisest. Of all who give and receive gifts, such as they are wisest. Everywhere they are wisest. They are the magi.

Commentary

Upon first reading, O. Henry's short story "The Gift of the Magi" may appear overly simple and perhaps heavy handed in its sermonizing. But what the reader of an O. Henry story needs to realize is that he utilizes to the point of perfection a delightful play on words, witty narration, and a twist ending that forces the reader to reevaluate the story. "The Gift of the Magi," especially, is one of his most popular stories that has reappeared in some form or other on celluloid, TV, in print, and in plays in the century since it was penned. What must be focused on, however, is the Biblical tradition of the story and the use of the homily in the last paragraph to give moral guidance rather than a religious sermon. O. Henry is not preaching, but giving moral counsel for all despite any religious affiliation.

The first Biblical tradition that appears not only in this story, but in many of O. Henry's, is the disparity between the rich and the poor. The story begins with an emphasis on the Young's poverty. $1.87, with a little less than half of that in pennies, is all they have in their name; don't forget that they also have to pay $8 for rent of a dilapidated apartment every week. Jim Young used to make $30 a week, but now only makes $20. They are so poor, in fact, that they have to bargain with shop venders to get a cheaper price, an indignity to a western mind. O. Henry makes a distinction of class when he introduces the male protagonist as Mr. James Dillingham Young, where Dillingham has a very aristocratic connotation. Since Jim has been demoted in pay, as if in response, "Dillingham" on the nameplate to his apartment has also faded, reducing him from an "upper-class citizen" to that of an ordinary citizen with the initial D. In fact, he is reduced to the intimate name of Jim for the rest of the story. O. Henry is clearly showing the power of names to segregate and discriminate between the classes.

However, O. Henry wants the reader to understand that money is not commensurate with riches. He uses the two Bible figures of Queen Sheba and King Solomon to highlight this idea. Both figures were noted for their monetary riches and riches in wisdom. Della's hair is compared to the riches of Queen Sheba, and Jim's gold watch is compared to the riches of King Solomon. If the two monarchs had possessed the two treasures of the story's protagonists, then they would have been the most valued of all they owned. But why would O. Henry refer to these two monarchs for a comparison?

Queen of Sheba is thought to have been queen of an ancient kingdom located in what is now modern Ethiopia and the western section of the Arabian Peninsula. Hearing of King Solomon's wisdom, she brought gold, spices, and precious stones to pay for a taste of his insight. She foreshadows the magi mentioned in this story as well, for her three gifts are a similar parallel to the magi's three gifts. What O. Henry seems to hint at throughout the story is the interrelationship between wisdom and riches. If this is so, then the Youngs are rich indeed.

King Solomon is the son of the infamous King David and Bathsheba in the Old Testament. When he became king, he prayed that God would grant him wisdom to rule the land righteously. God granted his prayer, and King Solomon became the wisest ruler in the land, where many from afar would come to benefit from his wisdom. From his blood lines would come the savior of the world, Jesus Christ, to whom the magi would travel over great distances to pay homage with gifts of gold, frankincense, and myrrh.

The second biblical tradition is the essence of gift-giving being a mirror to generosity. Most are familiar with the idea of gift giving. Christmas is such a time in western tradition where gifts are exchanged. Other holidays in the east, like New Years or Thanksgiving, also involve the giving of money to those who pay respect. The superficiality of such gift giving has often tarnished the true intent of generosity from the heart and not the wallet. What O. Henry has illustrated in this tale is a love so profound that it exceeds wisdom. Both Jim and Della sell their most precious treasures, treasures equaled to those of monarchs, to buy a gift that exceeded their own. Della's hair was the crown of her beauty, and Jim's watch was irreplaceable for it was the only thing inherited from his father. "Of all who give and receive gifts, such as they are wisest." These two surpass Solomon's wisdom, and Sheba's wealth, for they gave up the very things that define themselves to buy gifts that accentuated the very gifts they forsook.

The true gifts they give, then, are not the material, but the immaterial: love, the third Biblical tradition. First, each knows the other so well that they buy the very gift that will please the other. Second, when the very items the gifts were bought for were sold to buy the gifts, the couple harbors no ill feelings toward each other. When Jim says, "They're too nice to use just at present. I sold the watch to get the money to buy your combs," he seems to indicate the irony of gift giving. It is not the gift that matters but the intention behind the gift. How many can actually say that last gift given was done out of sacrifice? Have any gifts given ever been out of sacrifice? These are the questions that O. Henry seems to be asking by the time he writes the homily in the final paragraph.

The magi from the title of the story as well as the homily are central to understanding the story. Why are they wise? It was known that the magi were probably Zoroastrian because they were from the East and could read the signs in the sky. What made them wise were the very gifts that they brought: gold, frankincense, and myrrh. They travelled from another part of the world to bestow these fine gifts, though not of equal value as Queen Sheba's gold, spices, and precious stones. What they did bring were prophetic gifts. Like Jim and Della, who give gifts that indicate it is not what they own that matters, but each other; the magi, likewise, bear gifts that symbolized the role of Christ in all of humanity's life. Gold was, of course, given to kings, and symbolized that Christ was not only the King of Israel, but also the world. Myrrh, having no apparent value except as incense at funerals, may seem like an odd gift to bear a quarter of the way around the world, but it was a common ointment used for embalming and was commonly used by priests as a holy anointing oil. It was a medicine offered to Christ while on the cross to ease his pain and was actually used to prepare Christ's body for burial in the tomb. Frankincense was a resin also commonly used as incense and more importantly for anointing newborns on their journey into a new spiritual life. Symbolically it represents the new life that Jesus would be born into upon his resurrection.

Each gift may seem superficial or superfluous, but upon closer examination, the reader is forced to reevaluate the very nature of gift giving. "Eight dollars a week or a million a year—

what is the difference? A mathematician or a wit would give you the wrong answer. The magi brought valuable gifts, but that was not among them." O. Henry saw the magi as wise for they offered gifts as they should be, for the true gift of the magi is the intent of their gift and not the intrinsic value of it.

Introduction of the Author

Kate Chopin (1850-1904)

Catherine O'Flaherty was born on July 12, 1850 in St. Louis, Missouri, the youngest of three to an immigrant Irishman, Thomas O'Flaherty and a French-American mother, Eliza Faris. With the death of her father in 1855, Kate found herself living with a widowed mother, grandmother, and great-grandmother, all who were smart, independent women. That same year she entered the Sacred Heart Academy, a Catholic boarding school known for highly intelligent nuns, where she found a love for books, especially the writings of Sir Walter Scott and Charles Dickens. By the time she was thirteen, she decided to drop out of traditional school entirely and devote her own education to books. Such independence lasted only two years when she decided to return to Sacred Heart Academy. She graduated at the top of her class with a penchant for superb story telling.

In 1870, she married Oscar Chopin, who was a fair man of liberal thinking and afforded his new wife all the luxuries and freedom an intelligent, independent woman could want at the time. She was even known to walk through the city streets unaccompanied by her husband, which caused quite a stir amongst the locals. Oscar bought a cotton plantation, which he failed to manage effectively. By the time she was 28, she gave birth to five boys and two girls. Four years later Oscar died of swamp fever, leaving his widow and seven kids in considerable debt. Selling the plantation, Chopin moved in with her mother, only to see her die the next year. Forced to alternative means of making money, Chopin turned to writing, where she set her pen to the lifestyle and people she knew in Louisiana. She published her first novel, *At Fault,* in 1890, but had already started her writing career the previous year with the publication of three short stories. "The Story of an Hour," perhaps her most anthologized short story, was published in 1891. The focus of independent women in these stories shut editors off from her work, and she was forced to pay for the publication of her first novel out of her own funds.

Her highest critical acclaim came in 1894, with the publication of a collection of short stories in *Bayou Folk* that showcased the classical Chopin characters of self-reliant women struggling for purpose in a male dominated society. She followed the success of her first collection with a second in 1897, *A Night in Acadia,* which includes "A Respectable Woman," originally published in *Vogue* magazine in 1894. Yet it is with her most respected novel to date that shocked her conservative readers and gave her bad press. The Awakening, published in 1899, marked the turning point of her literary career by proving that she was a novelist worthy of remembrance; it is considered an American masterpiece now, but also ended her critical reputation and career as a writer. America at the time was not yet ready for the strong feminist viewpoint of Chopin or her novel's protagonist, Edna Pontellier, who "awakens" into the full independency and sexuality of womanhood that is applauded by readers today. The critical backlash surprised Chopin, which hurt her deeply, causing her to destroy the manuscript, and over the next five years, she only published a couple of short stories that were not paid much attention to.

Five years after her dismal failure, Kate Chopin died, forgotten and resentful, from a brain hemorrhage in 1904. Though her critics had managed to destroy her literary life, and her contemporary fans had abandoned her, Chopin's writing found renewed interest in the 1960's as the leading feminist voice of her time.

A Respectable Woman

Mrs. Baroda was a little provoked to learn that her husband expected his friend, Gouvernail, up to spend a week or two on the plantation.

They had entertained a good deal during the winter; much of the time had also been passed in New Orleans[1] in various forms of mild dissipation. She was looking forward to a period of unbroken rest, now, and undisturbed tete-a-tete[2] with her husband, when he informed her that Gouvernail was coming up to stay a week or two.

This was a man she had heard much of but never seen. He had been her husband's college friend; was now a journalist, and in no sense a society man or "a man about town," which were, perhaps, some of the reasons she had never met him. But she had unconsciously formed an image of him in her mind. She pictured him tall, slim, cynical; with eye-glasses, and his hands in his pockets; and she did not like him. Gouvernail was slim enough, but he wasn't very tall nor very cynical; neither did he wear eyeglasses nor carry his hands in his pockets. And she rather liked him when he first presented himself.

But why she liked him she could not explain satisfactorily to herself when she partly attempted to do so. She could discover in him none of those brilliant and promising traits which Gaston, her husband, had often assured her that he possessed. On the

---

1. **New Orleans**: a city in the southern tip of Louisiana, USA
2. **tete-a-tete**: a private conversation

contrary, he sat rather mute and receptive before her chatty eagerness to make him feel at home and in face of Gaston's frank and wordy hospitality. His manner was as courteous toward her as the most exacting woman could require; but he made no direct appeal to her approval or even esteem.

Once settled at the plantation he seemed to like to sit upon the wide portico[3] in the shade of one of the big Corinthian pillars,[4] smoking his cigar lazily and listening attentively to Gaston's experience as a sugar planter.

"This is what I call living," he would utter with deep satisfaction, as the air that swept across the sugar field caressed him with its warm and scented velvety touch. It pleased him also to get on familiar terms with the big dogs that came about him, rubbing themselves sociably against his legs. He did not care to fish, and displayed no eagerness to go out and kill grosbecs[5] when Gaston proposed doing so.

Gouvernail's personality puzzled Mrs. Baroda, but she liked him. Indeed, he was a lovable, inoffensive fellow. After a few days, when she could understand him no better than at first, she gave over being puzzled and remained piqued.[6] In this mood she left her husband and her guest, for the most part, alone together. Then finding that Gouvernail took no manner of exception to her action, she imposed her society upon him, accompanying him in his idle strolls to the mill and walks along the batture.[7] She persistently sought to penetrate the reserve in which he had uncon-

---

3. **portico**: a porch with a roof supported by columns
4. **Corinthian pillars**: a specific pillar with leaves, foliage, or different flowers decorating the capital, the top part of the pillar
5. **grosbec**: a variant of grosbeak; a type of finch bird with a conical bill
6. **piqued**: irritated
7. **batture**: elevated riverbed

sciously enveloped himself.

"When is he going—your friend?" she one day asked her husband. "For my part, he tires me frightfully."

"Not for a week yet, dear. I can't understand; he gives you no trouble."

"No. I should like him better if he did; if he were more like others, and I had to plan somewhat for his comfort and enjoyment."

Gaston took his wife's pretty face between his hands and looked tenderly and laughingly into her troubled eyes.

They were making a bit of toilet[8] sociably together in Mrs. Baroda's dressing-room.

"You are full of surprises, ma belle,[9]" he said to her. "Even I can never count upon how you are going to act under given conditions." He kissed her and turned to fasten his cravat[10] before the mirror.

"Here you are," he went on, "taking poor Gouvernail seriously and making a commotion over him, the last thing he would desire or expect."

"Commotion!" she hotly resented. "Nonsense! How can you say such a thing? Commotion, indeed! But, you know, you said he was clever."

"So he is. But the poor fellow is run down by overwork now. That's why I asked him here to take a rest."

"You used to say he was a man of ideas," she retorted, unconciliated.[11] "I expected him to be interesting, at least. I'm

---

8. **toilet**: the act of grooming and dressing
9. **ma belle**: affectionate French term meaning "honey"
10. **cravat**: necktie
11 **unconciliated**: not yet placated or reconciled

going to the city in the morning to have my spring gowns fitted. Let me know when Mr. Gouvernail is gone; I shall be at my Aunt Octavie's."

That night she went and sat alone upon a bench that stood beneath a live oak tree at the edge of the gravel walk.

She had never known her thoughts or her intentions to be so confused. She could gather nothing from them but the feeling of a distinct necessity to quit her home in the morning.

Mrs. Baroda heard footsteps crunching the gravel; but could discern in the darkness only the approaching red point of a lighted cigar. She knew it was Gouvernail, for her husband did not smoke. She hoped to remain unnoticed, but her white gown revealed her to him. He threw away his cigar and seated himself upon the bench beside her; without a suspicion that she might object to his presence.

"Your husband told me to bring this to you, Mrs. Baroda," he said, handing her a filmy, white scarf with which she sometimes enveloped her head and shoulders. She accepted the scarf from him with a murmur of thanks, and let it lie in her lap.

He made some commonplace observation upon the baneful effect of the night air at the season. Then as his gaze reached out into the darkness, he murmured, half to himself:

" 'Night of south winds—night of the large few stars!
Still nodding night—' "

She made no reply to this apostrophe[12] to the night, which, indeed, was not addressed to her.

---

12 **apostrophe**: address (to an imaginary person or thing)

Gouvernail was in no sense a diffident[13] man, for he was not a self-conscious one. His periods of reserve were not constitutional, but the result of moods. Sitting there beside Mrs. Baroda, his silence melted for the time.

He talked freely and intimately in a low, hesitating drawl that was not unpleasant to hear. He talked of the old college days when he and Gaston had been a good deal to each other; of the days of keen and blind ambitions and large intentions. Now there was left with him, at least, a philosophic acquiescence[14] to the existing order—only a desire to be permitted to exist, with now and then a little whiff of genuine life, such as he was breathing now.

Her mind only vaguely grasped what he was saying. Her physical being was for the moment predominant. She was not thinking of his words, only drinking in the tones of his voice. She wanted to reach out her hand in the darkness and touch him with the sensitive tips of her fingers upon the face or the lips. She wanted to draw close to him and whisper against his cheek—she did not care what—as she might have done if she had not been a respectable woman.

The stronger the impulse grew to bring herself near him, the further, in fact, did she draw away from him. As soon as she could do so without an appearance of too great rudeness, she rose and left him there alone.

Before she reached the house, Gouvernail had lighted a fresh cigar and ended his apostrophe to the night.

Mrs. Baroda was greatly tempted that night to tell her husband—who was also her friend—of this folly that had seized her.

---

13. diffident: shy
14. acquiescence: agreement

But she did not yield to the temptation. Beside being a respectable woman she was a very sensible one; and she knew there are some battles in life which a human being must fight alone.

When Gaston arose in the morning, his wife had already departed. She had taken an early morning train to the city. She did not return till Gouvernail was gone from under her roof.

There was some talk of having him back during the summer that followed. That is, Gaston greatly desired it; but this desire yielded to his wife's strenuous opposition.

However, before the year ended, she proposed, wholly from herself, to have Gouvernail visit them again. Her husband was surprised and delighted with the suggestion coming from her.

"I am glad, chere amie,[15] to know that you have finally overcome your dislike for him; truly he did not deserve it."

"Oh," she told him, laughingly, after pressing a long, tender kiss upon his lips, "I have overcome everything! you will see. This time I shall be very nice to him."

---

15 **chere amie**: affectionate French term meaning "dear friend"

Commentary

After reading Kate Chopin's "A Respectable Woman," some modern readers may wonder what the point of this rather unremarkable story is. A Victorian woman finds her husband's friend to be less than expected. Her husband pleads with her to like him. She meets with him and realizes her feelings for him are deeper and more intimate than before. Thus, she refuses to see him again as a respectable woman should do. A year passes and she decides to meet with him again, and "this time I shall be very nice to him," she replies. A devoted wife losing feelings for her husband and falling for a more romantic figure is a cliché in today's movies and romances. From a Victorian perspective, and the title of the story, passion was something a "respectable woman" was not allowed since marriages were mostly arranged out of convenience by fathers and future husbands for various reasons such as securing economic stability or class advancement. Kate Chopin, as evidenced in her stories and novels, found marriage of necessity a trap that women should not be consigned to.

The Victorian period, though ruled by Queen Victoria, did not offer women much freedom in marriage, to vote, or to do much outside of raising a family. Some women were satisfied with their station in life, others, like Chopin, found the need to express their own oppressive feelings through fiction and what it meant to be a woman. Most of what Chopin wrote dealt with themes of a woman's sexuality and her oppressive condition in marriage. In a time when women were not supposed to be sexual in nature—they were expected to participate in matrimonial intercourse for the purpose of having offspring and not for pleasure—Chopin felt it necessary to express the physical side of a wife's sexual desire. Unlike her later novel *The Awakening* that openly details a woman's sexual awakening, "A Respectable Woman" hints at the idea of passion that must be repressed because it is what society deemed desirable:

> "Her mind only vaguely grasped what he was saying. Her physical being was for the moment predominant. She was not thinking of his words, only drinking in the tones of his voice. She wanted to reach out her hand in the darkness and touch him with the sensitive tips of her fingers upon the face or the lips. She wanted to draw close to him and whisper against his cheek—she did not care what—as she might have done if she had not been a respectable woman."

Mrs. Baroda does all she can to flee the temptation of her passions. What is oppressive to her, and starts to become oppressive to the reader as well, is the fact that she fails to harbor the same emotions for her husband. In fact, it seems that she never did. She seems trapped in a marriage of convenience, void of passion. Gouvernail is the exact opposite of Mr. Baroda, who is talkative, frank, and likes to fish and hunt. Gouvernail, on the other hand, is a good listener, reserved, and poetic. The poem he quotes in the middle of the night is from Walt Whitman's "Song of Myself," section 21. His passion stirs her own. The climax of this story is that any "respectable woman" at the time would concede to her duty and continue on in an oppressed marriage, but not Mrs. Baroda.

Mrs. Baroda is a Chopin symbol of the New Woman, a woman that attempts to break free from the shackles of passionless marriage into relationships of passion. The New Woman no longer feels the need to have her life dictated by the whims of her calloused husband. This is the meaning behind the final sentence when she states she will finally be nice to her husband's friend. A Victorian story written by a male would have had the heroin ultimately reject her feelings for Gouvernail and return to her husband wholeheartedly. However, Mrs. Baroda chooses a life of passion and emotional equilibrium over that of being a respectable Victorian woman, which, to Kate Chopin, should be a thing of the past.

Introduction of the Author

Nathaniel Hawthorne (1804-1864)

Considered one of America's most important writers, as well as the most modern, Nathaniel Hawthorne was born in Salem, Massachusetts, on July 4, 1804. His father was a ship captain who had died at sea when he was four years old. After his father's death, his family moved in with his mother's parents in a country estate, where he read eagerly and fell in love with the countryside. He returned to Salem in 1821 to attend Bowdoin College where he met the three most important and influential friends in his life: Horatio Bridge, a later United States Naval officer, who helped Hawthorne publish his first book; Henry Wadsworth Longfellow, the later famed poet of "Hiawatha", who reviewed Hawthorne's first book; and Franklin Pierce, who would later become the 14th President of the United States.

After graduation, Hawthorne turned to writing; a profession that was not looked upon very well since most books were brought over from England, and most short story authors used pseudonyms to hide the fact that they actually worked in a low paying industry. His first novel, *Fanshawe* (1828) published under the pseudonym Peter Parley, drew upon his college experiences and was published using his own money. He then spent twelve lonely years writing and trying to make a name for himself in an industry that just did not care. Then in 1837, Hawthorne published *Twice-Told Tales*, a collection of his short stories that finally earned him his sought after recognition. Included in *Twice-Told Tales* is "Dr. Heidegger's Experiment" that was first published anonymously in the *Knickerbocker* magazine. Just to make money to support his writing lifestyle, however, Hawthorne started work at the Boston Custom House in 1839 that later led to his employment at the Salem Custom House in 1846, which is introduced in his most popular work, *The Scarlet Letter* (1850). By 1842, Hawthorne had earned enough money to marry Sophia Peabody, who was of similar temperament and loved his works of fiction. Though he later lost his job at the Salem Custom House when the country changed Presidents, he wrote a favorable campaign biography for his old friend Pierce, who was later elected President in 1852. As a reward for his help, Pierce appointed him Consul to Liverpool, improving his financial situation considerably.

Hawthorne wrote his most famous novels after 1850, which started with a lasting friendship with author Herman Melville of *Moby Dick* (1851) fame. Melville was a fan of Hawthorne's writing, especially his short story collection *Mosses from an Old Manse* (1846). He went on to write *The Scarlet Letter* (1850), *The House of the Seven Gables* (1851), *The Blithedale Romance* (1852), and *The Marble Faun* (1860), which was written while he lived in Italy, all recognized as great modern romances. Hawthorne also encouraged Melville to write his grand novel *Moby Dick*, which he dedicated to Hawthorne by writing, "In Token of my admiration for his genius, This book is inscribed to Nathaniel Hawthorne."

By 1860, Hawthorne's health was deteriorating that only accelerated with stress of the coming Civil War (1861-1865). Nathaniel Hawthorne died peacefully in his sleep on May 18, 1864, after traveling through the White Mountains, New Hampshire, with ex-president Piece.

Dr. Heidegger's Experiment

That very singular man, old Dr. Heidegger, once invited four venerable friends to meet him in his study. There were three white-bearded gentlemen, Mr. Medbourne, Colonel Killigrew, and Mr. Gascoigne, and a withered gentlewoman, whose name was the Widow Wycherly. They were all melancholy old creatures, who had been unfortunate in life, and whose greatest misfortune it was that they were not long ago in their graves. Mr. Medbourne, in the vigor of his age, had been a prosperous merchant, but had lost his all by a frantic speculation,[1] and was now little better than a mendicant.[2] Colonel Killigrew had wasted his best years, and his health and substance, in the pursuit of sinful pleasures, which had given birth to a brood[3] of pains, such as the gout,[4] and divers other torments of soul and body. Mr. Gascoigne was a ruined politician, a man of evil fame, or at least had been so till time had buried him from the knowledge of the present generation, and made him obscure instead of infamous. As for the Widow Wycherly, tradition tells us that she was a great beauty in her day; but, for a long while past, she had lived in deep seclusion, on account of certain scandalous stories which had prejudiced the gentry of the town against her. It is a circumstance worth mentioning that each of these three old gentlemen,

1. **speculation**: a get-rich-quick scheme that can actually work, or drain your profits
2. **mendicant**: beggar
3. **brood**: group
4. **gout**: a disease that causes pain in the joints

Mr. Medbourne, Colonel Killigrew, and Mr. Gascoigne, were early lovers of the Widow Wycherly, and had once been on the point of cutting each other's throats for her sake. And, before proceeding further, I will merely hint that Dr. Heidegger and all his foul guests were sometimes thought to be a little beside themselves,—as is not unfrequently the case with old people, when worried either by present troubles or woeful recollections.

"My dear old friends," said Dr. Heidegger, motioning them to be seated, "I am desirous of your assistance in one of those little experiments with which I amuse myself here in my study."

If all stories were true, Dr. Heidegger's study must have been a very curious place. It was a dim, old-fashioned chamber, festooned[5] with cobwebs, and besprinkled with antique dust. Around the walls stood several oaken bookcases, the lower shelves of which were filled with rows of gigantic folios and black-letter quartos,[6] and thc upper with little parchment-covered duodecimos.[7] Over the central bookcase was a bronze bust of Hippocrates,[8] with which, according to some authorities, Dr. Heidegger was accustomed to hold consultations in all difficult cases of his practice. In the obscurest corner of the room stood a tall and narrow oaken closet, with its door ajar, within which doubtfully appeared a skeleton. Between two of the bookcases hung a looking-glass, presenting its high and dusty plate within a tarnished gilt[9] frame. Among many wonderful stories related of this mirror, it was fabled that the spirits of all the doctor's deceased patients dwelt

---

5. **festooned**: covered
6. **quarto**: a book 1/4 size of a regular book
7. **duodecimo**: a book 1/12 the size of a regular book
8. **Hippocrates**: (460-377 B.C.) Greek physician considered the Father of Medicine
9. **gilt**: gold

within its verge, and would stare him in the face whenever he looked thitherward. The opposite side of the chamber was ornamented with the full-length portrait of a young lady, arrayed in the faded magnificence of silk, satin, and brocade, and with a visage as faded as her dress. Above half a century ago, Dr. Heidegger had been on the point of marriage with this young lady; but, being affected with some slight disorder, she had swallowed one of her lover's prescriptions, and died on the bridal evening. The greatest curiosity of the study remains to be mentioned; it was a ponderous folio volume, bound in black leather, with massive silver clasps. There were no letters on the back, and nobody could tell the title of the book. But it was well known to be a book of magic; and once, when a chambermaid had lifted it, merely to brush away the dust, the skeleton had rattled in its closet, the picture of the young lady had stepped one foot upon the floor, and several ghastly faces had peeped forth from the mirror; while the brazen head of Hippocrates frowned, and said,—"Forbear!"[10]

Such was Dr. Heidegger's study. On the summer afternoon of our tale a small round table, as black as ebony, stood in the centre of the room, sustaining a cut-glass vase of beautiful form and elaborate workmanship. The sunshine came through the window, between the heavy festoons of two faded damask curtains,[11] and fell directly across this vase; so that a mild splendor was reflected from it on the ashen visages of the five old people who sat around. Four champagne glasses were also on the table.

"My dear old friends," repeated Dr. Heidegger, "may I reckon on your aid in performing an exceedingly curious experiment?"

Now Dr. Heidegger was a very strange old gentleman,

---

10. **forbear**: stop

11. **damask curtains**: curtains with rich designs woven into the cloth

whose eccentricity had become the nucleus for a thousand fantastic stories. Some of these fables, to my shame be it spoken, might possibly be traced back to my own veracious[12] self; and if any passages of the present tale should startle the reader's faith, I must be content to bear the stigma of a fiction monger.

When the doctor's four guests heard him talk of his proposed experiment, they anticipated nothing more wonderful than the murder of a mouse in an air pump, or the examination of a cobweb by the microscope, or some similar nonsense, with which he was constantly in the habit of pestering his intimates. But without waiting for a reply, Dr. Heidegger hobbled across the chamber, and returned with the same ponderous folio, bound in black leather, which common report affirmed to be a book of magic. Undoing the silver clasps, he opened the volume, and took from among its black-letter pages a rose, or what was once a rose, though now the green leaves and crimson petals had assumed one brownish hue, and the ancient flower seemed ready to crumble to dust in the doctor's hands.

"This rose," said Dr. Heidegger, with a sigh, "this same withered and crumbling flower, blossomed five and fifty years ago. It was given me by Sylvia Ward, whose portrait hangs yonder; and I meant to wear it in my bosom at our wedding. Five and fifty years it has been treasured between the leaves of this old volume. Now, would you deem it possible that this rose of half a century could ever bloom again?"

"Nonsense!" said the Widow Wycherly, with a peevish toss of her head. "You might as well ask whether an old woman's wrinkled face could ever bloom again."

"See!" answered Dr. Heidegger.

---

12. **veracious**: truthful

He uncovered the vase, and threw the faded rose into the water which it contained. At first, it lay lightly on the surface of the fluid, appearing to imbibe[13] none of its moisture. Soon, however, a singular change began to be visible. The crushed and dried petals stirred, and assumed a deepening tinge of crimson, as if the flower were reviving from a deathlike slumber; the slender stalk and twigs of foliage became green; and there was the rose of half a century, looking as fresh as when Sylvia Ward had first given it to her lover. It was scarcely full blown; for some of its delicate red leaves curled modestly around its moist bosom, within which two or three dewdrops were sparkling.

"That is certainly a very pretty deception," said the doctor's friends; carelessly, however, for they had witnessed greater miracles at a conjurer's show; "pray how was it effected?"

"Did you never hear of the 'Fountain of Youth?' " asked Dr. Heidegger, "which Ponce De Leon,[14] the Spanish adventurer, went in search of two or three centuries ago?"

"But did Ponce De Leon ever find it?" said the Widow Wycherly.

"No," answered Dr. Heidegger, "for he never sought it in the right place. The famous Fountain of Youth, if I am rightly informed, is situated in the southern part of the Floridian peninsula, not far from Lake Macaco. Its source is overshadowed by several gigantic magnolias, which, though numberless centuries old, have been kept as fresh as violets by the virtues of this wonderful water. An acquaintance of mine, knowing my curiosity in

---

13. **imbibe**: drink
14. **Ponce De Leon**: (1460-1521) Spanish explorer who sailed with Columbus on his second voyage and discovered the state of Florida while searching for the Fountain of Youth

such matters, has sent me what you see in the vase."

"Ahem!" said Colonel Killigrew, who believed not a word of the doctor's story; "and what may be the effect of this fluid on the human frame?"

"You shall judge for yourself, my dear colonel," replied Dr. Heidegger; "and all of you, my respected friends, are welcome to so much of this admirable fluid as may restore to you the bloom of youth. For my own part, having had much trouble in growing old, I am in no hurry to grow young again. With your permission, therefore, I will merely watch the progress of the experiment."

While he spoke, Dr. Heidegger had been filling the four champagne glasses with the water of the Fountain of Youth. It was apparently impregnated with an effervescent[15] gas, for little bubbles were continually ascending from the depths of the glasses, and bursting in silvery spray at the surface. As the liquor diffused a pleasant perfume, the old people doubted not that it possessed cordial and comfortable properties; and though utter skeptics as to its rejuvenescent[16] power, they were inclined to swallow it at once. But Dr. Heidegger besought them to stay a moment.

"Before you drink, my respectable old friends," said he, "it would be well that, with the experience of a lifetime to direct you, you should draw up a few general rules for your guidance, in passing a second time through the perils of youth. Think what a sin and shame it would be, if, with your peculiar advantages, you should not become patterns of virtue and wisdom to all the young people of the age!"

---

15. **effervescent**: bubbling
16. **rejuvenescent**: make young again

The doctor's four venerable friends made him no answer, except by a feeble and tremulous laugh; so very ridiculous was the idea that, knowing how closely repentance treads behind the steps of error, they should ever go astray again.

"Drink, then," said the doctor, bowing: "I rejoice that I have so well selected the subjects of my experiment."

With palsied[17] hands, they raised the glasses to their lips. The liquor, if it really possessed such virtues as Dr. Heidegger imputed to it, could not have been bestowed on four human beings who needed it more woefully. They looked as if they had never known what youth or pleasure was, but had been the offspring of Nature's dotage,[18] and always the gray, decrepit, sapless, miserable creatures, who now sat stooping round the doctor's table, without life enough in their souls or bodies to be animated even by the prospect of growing young again. They drank off the water, and replaced their glasses on the table.

Assuredly there was an almost immediate improvement in the aspect of the party, not unlike what might have been produced by a glass of generous wine, together with a sudden glow of cheerful sunshine brightening over all their visages at once. There was a healthful suffusion[19] on their cheeks, instead of the ashen hue that had made them look so corpse-like. They gazed at one another, and fancied that some magic power had really begun to smooth away the deep and sad inscriptions which Father Time had been so long engraving on their brows. The Widow Wycherly adjusted her cap, for she felt almost like a woman again.

---

17. **palsied**: difficult to move
18. **dotage**: old age; senility
19. **suffusion**: color

"Give us more of this wondrous water!" cried they, eagerly. "We are younger—but we are still too old! Quick—give us more!"

"Patience, patience!" quoth Dr. Heidegger, who sat watching the experiment with philosophic coolness. "You have been a long time growing old. Surely, you might be content to grow young in half an hour! But the water is at your service."

Again he filled their glasses with the liquor of youth, enough of which still remained in the vase to turn half the old people in the city to the age of their own grandchildren. While the bubbles were yet sparkling on the brim, the doctor's four guests snatched their glasses from the table, and swallowed the contents at a single gulp. Was it delusion? Even while the draught was passing down their throats, it seemed to have wrought a change on their whole systems. Their eyes grew clear and bright; a dark shade deepened among their silvery locks, they sat around the table, three gentlemen of middle age, and a woman, hardly beyond her buxom[20] prime.

"My dear widow, you are charming!" cried Colonel Killigrew, whose eyes had been fixed upon her face, while the shadows of age were flitting from it like darkness from the crimson daybreak.

The fair widow knew, of old, that Colonel Killigrew's compliments were not always measured by sober truth; so she started up and ran to the mirror, still dreading that the ugly visage of an old woman would meet her gaze. Meanwhile, the three gentlemen behaved in such a manner as proved that the water of the Fountain of Youth possessed some intoxicating qualities; unless, indeed, their exhilaration of spirits were merely a lightsome dizziness caused by the sudden removal of the weight of years. Mr.

20. **buxom**: healthy

Gascoigne's mind seemed to run on political topics, but whether relating to the past, present, or future, could not easily be determined, since the same ideas and phrases have been in vogue these fifty years. Now he rattled forth full-throated sentences about patriotism, national glory, and the people's right; now he muttered some perilous stuff or other, in a sly and doubtful whisper, so cautiously that even his own conscience could scarcely catch the secret; and now, again, he spoke in measured accents, and a deeply deferential tone, as if a royal ear were listening to his wellturned periods. Colonel Killigrew all this time had been trolling[21] forth a jolly bottle song, and ringing his glass in symphony with the chorus, while his eyes wandered toward the buxom[22] figure of the Widow Wycherly. On the other side of the table, Mr. Medbourne was involved in a calculation of dollars and cents, with which was strangely intermingled a project for supplying the East Indies with ice, by harnessing a team of whales to the polar icebergs.

As for the Widow Wycherly, she stood before the mirror curtseying and simpering to her own image, and greeting it as the friend whom she loved better than all the world beside. She thrust her face close to the glass, to see whether some long-remembered wrinkle or crow's foot had indeed vanished. She examined whether the snow had so entirely melted from her hair that the venerable cap could be safely thrown aside. At last, turning briskly away, she came with a sort of dancing step to the table.

"My dear old doctor," cried she, "pray favor me with another glass!"

---

21. **trolling**: singing
22. **buxom**: (different meaning from above) large breasted

"Certainly, my dear madam, certainly!" replied the complaisant doctor; "see! I have already filled the glasses."

There, in fact, stood the four glasses, brimful of this wonderful water, the delicate spray of which, as it effervesced from the surface, resembled the tremulous glitter of diamonds. It was now so nearly sunset that the chamber had grown duskier than ever; but a mild and moonlike splendor gleamed from within the vase, and rested alike on the four guests and on the doctor's venerable figure. He sat in a high-backed, elaborately-carved, oaken arm-chair, with a gray dignity of aspect that might have well befitted that very Father Time, whose power had never been disputed, save by this fortunate company. Even while quaffing[23] the third draught of the Fountain of Youth, they were almost awed by the expression of his mysterious visage.

But, the next moment, the exhilarating gush of young life shot through their veins. They were now in the happy prime of youth. Age, with its miserable train of cares and sorrows and diseases, was remembered only as the trouble of a dream, from which they had joyously awoke. The fresh gloss of the soul, so early lost, and without which the world's successive scenes had been but a gallery of faded pictures, again threw its enchantment over all their prospects. They felt like new-created beings in a new-created universe.

"We are young! We are young!" they cried exultingly.

Youth, like the extremity of age, had effaced the strongly-marked characteristics of middle life, and mutually assimilated them all. They were a group of merry youngsters, almost maddened with the exuberant frolicsomeness of their years. The most singular effect of their gayety was an impulse to mock the in-

---

23. **quaffing**: drinking deeply

firmity and decrepitude of which they had so lately been the victims. They laughed loudly at their old-fashioned attire, the wide-skirted coats and flapped waistcoats of the young men, and the ancient cap and gown of the blooming girl. One limped across the floor like a gouty grandfather; one set a pair of spectacles astride of his nose, and pretended to pore over the black-letter pages of the book of magic; a third seated himself in an arm-chair, and strove to imitate the venerable dignity of Dr. Heidegger. Then all shouted mirthfully, and leaped about the room. The Widow Wycherly—if so fresh a damsel could be called a widow—tripped up to the doctor's chair, with a mischievous merriment in her rosy face.

"Doctor, you dear old soul," cried she, "get up and dance with me!" And then the four young people laughed louder than ever, to think what a queer figure the poor old doctor would cut.

"Pray excuse me," answered the doctor quietly. "I am old and rheumatic,[24] and my dancing days were over long ago. But either of these gay young gentlemen will be glad of so pretty a partner."

"Dance with me, Clara!" cried Colonel Killigrew

"No, no, I will be her partner!" shouted Mr. Gascoigne.

"She promised me her hand, fifty years ago!" exclaimed Mr. Medbourne.

They all gathered round her. One caught both her hands in his passionate grasp another threw his arm about her waist—the third buried his hand among the glossy curls that clustered beneath the widow's cap. Blushing, panting, struggling, chiding, laughing, her warm breath fanning each of their faces by turns, she strove to disengage herself, yet still remained in their triple

---

24. **rheumatic**: suffering from pain in the back

embrace. Never was there a livelier picture of youthful rivalship, with bewitching beauty for the prize. Yet, by a strange deception, owing to the duskiness of the chamber, and the antique dresses which they still wore, the tall mirror is said to have reflected the figures of the three old, gray, withered grandsires, ridiculously contending for the skinny ugliness of a shriveled grandam.[25]

But they were young: their burning passions proved them so. Inflamed to madness by the coquetry[26] of the girl-widow, who neither granted nor quite withheld her favors, the three rivals began to interchange threatening glances. Still keeping hold of the fair prize, they grappled fiercely at one another's throats. As they struggled to and fro, the table was overturned, and the vase dashed into a thousand fragments. The precious Water of Youth flowed in a bright stream across the floor, moistening the wings of a butterfly, which, grown old in the decline of summer, had alighted there to die. The insect fluttered lightly through the chamber, and settled on the snowy head of Dr. Heidegger.

"Come, come, gentlemen!—come, Madam Wycherly," exclaimed the doctor, "I really must protest against this riot."

They stood still and shivered; for it seemed as if gray Time were calling them back from their sunny youth, far down into the chill and darksome vale of years. They looked at old Dr. Heidegger, who sat in his carved arm-chair, holding the rose of half a century, which he had rescued from among the fragments of the shattered vase. At the motion of his hand, the four rioters resumed their seats; the more readily, because their violent exertions had wearied them, youthful though they were.

"My poor Sylvia's rose!" ejaculated Dr. Heidegger, holding

---

25. **grandam**: grandma
26. **coquetry**: flirting

it in the light of the sunset clouds; "it appears to be fading again."

And so it was. Even while the party were looking at it, the flower continued to shrivel up, till it became as dry and fragile as when the doctor had first thrown it into the vase. He shook off the few drops of moisture which clung to its petals.

"I love it as well thus as in its dewy freshness," observed he, pressing the withered rose to his withered lips. While he spoke, the butterfly fluttered down from the doctor's snowy head, and fell upon the floor.

His guests shivered again. A strange chillness, whether of the body or spirit they could not tell, was creeping gradually over them all. They gazed at one another, and fancied that each fleeting moment snatched away a charm, and left a deepening furrow where none had been before. Was it an illusion? Had the changes of a lifetime been crowded into so brief a space, and were they now four aged people, sitting with their old friend, Dr. Heidegger?

"Are we grown old again, so soon?" cried they, dolefully.

In truth they had. The Water of Youth possessed merely a virtue more transient[27] than that of wine. The delirium which it created had effervesced away. Yes! they were old again. With a shuddering impulse, that showed her a woman still, the widow clasped her skinny hands before her face, and wished that the coffin lid were over it, since it could be no longer beautiful.

"Yes, friends, ye[28] are old again," said Dr. Heidegger, "and lo! the Water of Youth is all lavished on the ground. Well—I be-

---

27. **transient**: not permanent; short in time

28. **ye**: an elevated form of "you" used when addressing a group

moan it not; for if the fountain gushed at my very doorstep, I would not stoop to bathe my lips in it—no, though its delirium were for years instead of moments. Such is the lesson ye have taught me!"

But the doctor's four friends had taught no such lesson to themselves. They resolved forthwith to make a pilgrimage to Florida, and quaff at morning, noon, and night, from the Fountain of Youth.

Commentary

Upon first reading this light, airy story, readers may feel it a bit simplistic and outdated. Indeed the style of short story writing has changed significantly since then; however, the power this story still holds and the precision with which it is executed are hard to match. Hawthorne often wrote stories dealing with ethical criticism, the immorality of science, and its ill effects. His stories deal with a philosophical concept that is now dubbed "the double power principle." Developed by philosopher Tom Morris (1952–), the double power principle details that the more potential an invention has for good, it also has an equal potential for ill. A modern day example is nuclear energy. It has potential for cheap, clean production, but on the other hand, it can destroy entire nations, even the world. The double power principle works well to understand Hawthorne's concept of science. It can be the source of great miracles, or it can cause unimaginable harm. Hawthorne gives the reader an example of how such science has the ability to heal and scar through the four elderly characters in "Dr. Heidegger's Experiment."

First, the intent of Dr. Heidegger must be examined. He is not the typical "mad scientist." He is, instead, sober and conscientious of his own experiments. Hawthorne does surround him in mystery and mysticism through the painstaking description of the doctor's laboratory: the mirror haunted by his dead patients, a portrait of his lover whom he accidentally poisoned, and references to his magical book that had caused a skeleton to "rattle in its closet, the picture of the young lady had stepped one foot upon the floor, and several ghastly faces had peeped forth from the mirror." It is in these surroundings that Dr. Heidegger proposes his experiment. Naturally, he refuses to conduct the experiment on himself and settles for his four unwitting guinea pigs: the Widow Wycherly, Colonel Killigrew, Mr. Medbourne, and Mr. Gascoigne.

The Widow Wycherly is a recluse on account of her ruined reputation as a wanton mistress. At one time she was quite beautiful and swelled under the attention men paid to her. Even the three gentlemen present fought for the hand of the Widow Wycherly, and even would have killed to be with her. Only with age and the loss of that beauty did her popularity turn to infamy and shame, forcing her to become a secluded widow shut away from the eyes and mouths of the public. With the reversion to her youth, she sets about preening like a peacock and attracting the attentions of the three gentlemen yet again. They set to fighting over her, though it causes her some pain, and she cannot help but enjoy the attention she is receiving once again. All the while, the mirror reflects their true inner nature of still being old and ugly.

Colonel Killigrew is an elderly man who spent his youth chasing women and in sinful pleasures only to suffer for it in his later years. It is clear that in his old age he regrets the earlier carefree lifestyle that afflicts him presently with constant pain. When Dr. Heidegger offers him the water of the fountain of youth, he reverts to his old rapacious self, having learned nothing from his old age. Upon seeing the Widow Wycherly become young again, he compliments her upon her beauty and reverts back to his flirtatious ways, singing and ogling the beautifying widow.

Mr. Medbourne is a pauper who had once been a rather

wealthy merchant. He lost all his money by investing in crazy get rich quick schemes that drained his funds to the point of poverty. Upon his return to youth, his mind settles upon an extravagant scheme to spend the last of his pennies to supply "the East Indies with ice, by harnessing a team of whales to the polar icebergs." In other words, he has failed to learn from the follies of his youth.

Mr. Gascoigne is a disgraced politician who can only show his face in public now because he has been long forgotten. When he becomes young again, he sets forth speaking in pomp and circumstance that no one around, not even himself, can understand. Not only is he proud of speaking in useless political riddles, but no one so much as listens to his rants.

The double power principle comes into play through the very means the four "gray, withered, and shriveled" grandsires and grandam fail to learn from the mistakes of their youth. Each suffer in some form or other in their old age. Dr. Heidegger's experiment is to see if, given a second chance, his four friends would repent of their past misdeeds. The fountain of youth has the power to restore what has been lost, reverse time to the flower of youth, and to change the outward appearance to what it once was; however, it does not have the power to change what is inside. The experiment was a success. It changed each person physically back to his or her prime, yet it failed to open their eyes to their moral sickness. As with all things powerful, it is not the concept that is dangerous, but how a person uses it that is. The four take a seemingly innocent power and abuse it with their ignorance. Not only do they unwittingly destroy the very source of their youth, they fail to learn the lesson Dr. Heidegger did: mainly that old age and death is also a double power principle. Though death is final and fearsome, it does, through natural selection, bring an end to pride, rapaciousness, stupidity, and corruption. The doctor recognizes this and sees old age and death as the natural order of things. The four foolish friends do not. They will hunt down the source of their youth to forever live in ignorance that is the very source to their suffering and pain.

Introduction of the Author

Ambrose Bierce (1842-1913?)

American journalist and satirist Ambrose Bierce was born in Ohio and raised in Indiana. Born tenth in a large American family of thirteen, Ambrose often retreated to his father's large library to read. His father, Marcus Aurelius, named after the Roman Emperor, seemed to have a satirical slight that rubbed off onto young Ambrose and named each of his thirteen children starting with the letter A. He eventually moved his family to a farm in Indiana to keep his children occupied, an idea that Ambrose did not seem too fond of. In his satirical work *The Devil's Dictionary* (1911), Ambrose defines marriage as "The state or condition of a community consisting of a master, a mistress and two slaves, making in all, two." Because of his family's poverty, Ambrose mostly educated himself through books, and finished only one year of high school before he went on to apprentice as a printer at an antislavery newspaper at the age of fifteen. He was an ardent supporter of freeing the slaves and even fought for it.

When the American Civil War (1861-1865) broke out, Ambrose joined the Union Army of the north and quickly rose in rank to lieutenant; his idealism and patriotism drove him through the early campaigns of the war. His experience in the war lent fuel to his writing fire as many of his later stories featured the horrors of the war. He fought in some of the bloodiest and harshest battles of the war and survived. In June of 1864, he did get shot in the temple of his head with the bullet embedded into his skull behind his left ear. He recovered from his wound and soon went on to fight in other campaigns. However, in 1862, during the battle of Chickamuga, when all the senior offers fled the battle, Ambrose realized the war was madness, run by ignorant fools. It was perhaps at this time that Ambrose became the satirical cynic the world would later know him as.

After the war, Ambrose continued to write for various newspapers and soon landed an editorial position. In 1871, he published his first story, "The Haunted Valley." Though he was engaged during the war and had it broken off, Ambrose proposed to another, Mollie Day, and at the age of 29, he married her. They had three children, Day (1872–1889) Leigh (1874–1901), and Helen (1875–1940). The next year they moved to England where they lived for three years in London, so he could write for British magazines. During this time, he had published several volumes of sketches, but he became highly recognized for *Tales of Soldiers and Civilians* (1891), a collection of short stories about the Civil War, which includes his most famous story, "An Occurrence at Owl Creek Bridge." In 1877, he returned to San Francisco to write for a local paper and continue writing his satirical commentaries and sketches, earning the name "Bitter Bierce."

Ambrose separated from Mollie in 1888 and finally divorced her 17 years later. Such bitterness over relationships and marriage found vent in *The Devil's Dictionary* with such satirical entries like this one on love: "A temporary insanity curable by marriage;" preceded by another entry on helpmate: "A wife, or bitter half."

Though his stories are seen as rugged and masculine, Ambrose is regarded as the voice of late 19th century American literature by many critics with his writing accorded as being sophisticated of word and cautious in style by his contemporaries. He wrote several collections of poetry but is best remembered for his satire, which is often regarded as Swiftian, and though he wrote novels, he preferred the short story form best. He had such a wide range of styles, from civil war stories to horror, that he has been likened to Edgar Allan Poe, whose writing he rather disliked. In fact he wrote often in the popular early 20th century convention of grotesquerie, a type of horror where characters are either deranged physically or spiritually while performing profane deeds. More often than not, the characters in a grotesquerie novel or story are animalistic and the style is highly satiric, which Ambrose reveled in.

As his marriage started to fall apart, Ambrose became a heavy drinker. His son Day ran away from home at the age of fifteen and killed the rival suitor of a girl he wished to marry. Two years later, Day was killed in a duel. Ambrose continued to write and turn his satirical judgment on the world. He caused many scandals; one where a critical poem of the governor of Kentucky appeared to foreshadow his assassination. The paper he wrote for was accused of instigating the assassination, but he never lost his job. In 1913, Ambrose retired to Mexico, where he disappeared without a trace during a civil war called the Mexican Revolution (1910-1917). Only rumor and speculation surround his death. Many think he died during the war that he joined as an observer. Some even speculated he shot himself in the head near the Grand Canyon; others think he was taken captive by Brazilian natives. Despite his demise, he lived a grand life that is testament to his legacy as a great American writer.

An Occurrence at Owl Creek Bridge

Chapter I

A man stood upon a railroad bridge in northern Alabama, looking down into the swift water twenty feet below. The man's hands were behind his back, the wrists bound with a cord. A rope closely encircled his neck. It was attached to a stout cross-timber above his head and the slack fell to the level of his knees. Some loose boards laid upon the ties supporting the rails of the railway supplied a footing for him and his executioners—two private soldiers of the Federal army,[1] directed by a sergeant who in civil life may have been a deputy sheriff. At a short remove upon the same temporary platform was an officer in the uniform of his rank, armed. He was a captain. A sentinel[2] at each end of the bridge stood with his rifle in the position known as "support," that is to say, vertical in front of the left shoulder, the hammer resting on the forearm thrown straight across the chest—a formal and unnatural position, enforcing an erect carriage of the body. It did not appear to be the duty of these two men to know what was occurring at the center of the bridge; they merely blockaded the two ends of the foot planking that traversed it.

Beyond one of the sentinels nobody was in sight; the railroad ran straight away into a forest for a hundred yards, then, curving, was lost to view. Doubtless there was an outpost farther

---

1. **Federal army**: the northern army of Abraham Lincoln
2. **sentinel**: guard

along. The other bank of the stream was open ground—a gentle slope topped with a stockade of vertical tree trunks, loopholed for rifles, with a single embrasure[3] through which protruded the muzzle of a brass cannon commanding the bridge. Midway up the slope between the bridge and fort were the spectators—a single company of infantry in line, at "parade rest," the butts of their rifles on the ground, the barrels inclining slightly backward against the right shoulder, the hands crossed upon the stock. A lieutenant stood at the right of the line, the point of his sword upon the ground, his left hand resting upon his right. Excepting the group of four at the center of the bridge, not a man moved. The company faced the bridge, staring stonily, motionless. The sentinels, facing the banks of the stream, might have been statues to adorn the bridge. The captain stood with folded arms, silent, observing the work of his subordinates, but making no sign. Death is a dignitary who when he comes announced is to be received with formal manifestations of respect, even by those most familiar with him. In the code of military etiquette silence and fixity are forms of deference.[4]

The man who was engaged in being hanged was apparently about thirty-five years of age. He was a civilian, if one might judge from his habit, which was that of a planter. His features were good—a straight nose, firm mouth, broad forehead, from which his long, dark hair was combed straight back, falling behind his ears to the collar of his well fitting frock coat.[5] He wore a moustache and pointed beard, but no whiskers; his eyes were

---

3. **embrasure**: loophole; opening in a fortification through which a soldier can shoot a cannon or gun
4. **deference**: yielding; submission
5. **frock coat**: a snug, knee length coat worn by the gentry

large and dark gray, and had a kindly expression which one would hardly have expected in one whose neck was in the hem p.[6] Evidently this was no vulgar assassin. The liberal military code makes provision for hanging many kinds of persons, and gentlemen are not excluded.

The preparations being complete, the two private soldiers stepped aside and each drew away the plank upon which he had been standing. The sergeant turned to the captain, saluted and placed himself immediately behind that officer, who in turn moved apart one pace. These movements left the condemned man and the sergeant standing on the two ends of the same plank, which spanned three of the cross-ties of the bridge. The end upon which the civilian stood almost, but not quite, reached a fourth. This plank had been held in place by the weight of the captain; it was now held by that of the sergeant. At a signal from the former the latter would step aside, the plank would tilt and the condemned man go down between two ties. The arrangement commended itself to his judgment as simple and effective. His face had not been covered nor his eyes bandaged. He looked a moment at his "unsteadfast footing," then let his gaze wander to the swirling water of the stream racing madly beneath his feet. A piece of dancing driftwood caught his attention and his eyes followed it down the current. How slowly it appeared to move! What a sluggish stream!

He closed his eyes in order to fix his last thoughts upon his wife and children. The water, touched to gold by the early sun, the brooding mists under the banks at some distance down the stream, the fort, the soldiers, the piece of drift—all had distracted him. And now he became conscious of a new disturbance.

---

6. **hemp**: tough fiber from which rope is made; rope

Striking through the thought of his dear ones was sound which he could neither ignore nor understand, a sharp, distinct, metallic percussion like the stroke of a blacksmith's hammer upon the anvil; it had the same ringing quality. He wondered what it was, and whether immeasurably distant or near by—it seemed both. Its recurrence was regular, but as slow as the tolling of a death knell.[7] He awaited each new stroke with impatience and—he knew not why—apprehension. The intervals of silence grew progressively longer; the delays became maddening. With their greater infrequency the sounds increased in strength and sharpness. They hurt his ear like the thrust of a knife; he feared he would shriek. What he heard was the ticking of his watch.

He unclosed his eyes and saw again the water below him. "If I could free my hands," he thought, "I might throw off the noose and spring into the stream. By diving I could evade the bullets and, swimming vigorously, reach the bank, take to the woods and get away home. My home, thank God, is as yet outside their lines; my wife and little ones are still beyond the invader's farthest advance."

As these thoughts, which have here to be set down in words, were flashed into the doomed man's brain rather than evolved from it the captain nodded to the sergeant. The sergeant stepped aside.

Chapter II

Peyton Fahrquhar was a well to do planter, of an old and highly respected Alabama family. Being a slave owner and like

---

7. **death knell**: bell rung at a funeral

other slave owners a politician, he was naturally an original secessionist[8] and ardently devoted to the Southern cause. Circumstances of an imperious nature, which it is unnecessary to relate here, had prevented him from taking service with that gallant army which had fought the disastrous campaigns ending with the fall of Corinth,[9] and he chafed[10] under the inglorious restraint, longing for the release of his energies, the larger life of the soldier, the opportunity for distinction. That opportunity, he felt, would come, as it comes to all in wartime. Meanwhile he did what he could. No service was too humble for him to perform in the aid of the South,[11] no adventure too perilous for him to undertake if consistent with the character of a civilian who was at heart a soldier, and who in good faith and without too much qualification assented to at least a part of the frankly villainous dictum[12] that all is fair in love and war.

One evening while Fahrquhar and his wife were sitting on a rustic bench near the entrance to his grounds, a gray-clad soldier rode up to the gate and asked for a drink of water. Mrs. Fahrquhar was only too happy to serve him with her own white hands. While she was fetching the water her husband approached the dusty horseman and inquired eagerly for news from the front.

"The Yanks[13] are repairing the railroads," said the man,

---

8. **secessionist**: those who supported the southern states breaking away from the United States before and during the American Civil War
9. **fall of Corinth**: a major battle fought in Mississippi, ending with the northern Federal army victorious
10. **chafe**: become irritated
11. **South**: the southern American states that wished to break away from the northern Federal states, wishing to retain their right to own slaves
12. **dictum**: saying; maxim

"and are getting ready for another advance. They have reached the Owl Creek bridge, put it in order and built a stockade on the north bank. The commandant has issued an order, which is posted everywhere, declaring that any civilian caught interfering with the railroad, its bridges, tunnels, or trains will be summarily hanged. I saw the order."

"How far is it to the Owl Creek bridge?"

Fahrquhar asked.

"About thirty miles."

"Is there no force on this side of the creek?"

"Only a picket post half a mile out, on the railroad, and a single sentinel at this end of the bridge."

"Suppose a man—a civilian and student of hanging—should elude the picket post and perhaps get the better of the sentinel," said Fahrquhar, smiling, "what could he accomplish?"

The soldier reflected. "I was there a month ago," he replied. "I observed that the flood of last winter had lodged a great quantity of driftwood against the wooden pier at this end of the bridge. It is now dry and would burn like tinder."

The lady had now brought the water, which the soldier drank. He thanked her ceremoniously, bowed to her husband and rode away. An hour later, after nightfall, he repassed[14] the plantation,[15] going northward in the direction from which he had come. He was a Federal scout.[16]

---

13. **Yanks**: the northern American states that wished to abolish slavery and supported the federal government
14. **repass**: to pass back the opposite direction originally gone
15. **plantation**: large estates that grow, in the South, cotton and maintained by slave labor. Thus, one of the factors of the Civil War was economic; without slaves, many of these plantations would and did fail to prosper
16. **Federal scout**: a spy for the Federal army

Chapter III

As Peyton Fahrquhar fell straight downward through the bridge he lost consciousness and was as one already dead. From this state he was awakened—ages later, it seemed to him—by the pain of a sharp pressure upon his throat, followed by a sense of suffocation. Keen, poignant agonies seemed to shoot from his neck downward through every fiber of his body and limbs. These pains appeared to flash along well defined lines of ramification and to beat with an inconceivably rapid periodicity. They seemed like streams of pulsating fire heating him to an intolerable temperature. As to his head, he was conscious of nothing but a feeling of fullness—of congestion. These sensations were unaccompanied by thought. The intellectual part of his nature was already effaced;[17] he had power only to feel, and feeling was torment. He was conscious of motion. Encompassed in a luminous cloud, of which he was now merely the fiery heart, without material substance, he swung through unthinkable arcs of oscillation, like a vast pendulum. Then all at once, with terrible suddenness, the light about him shot upward with the noise of a loud splash; a frightful roaring was in his ears, and all was cold and dark. The power of thought was restored; he knew that the rope had broken and he had fallen into the stream. There was no additional strangulation; the noose about his neck was already suffocating him and kept the water from his lungs. To die of hanging at the bottom of a river!—the idea seemed to him ludicrous. He opened his eyes in the darkness and saw above him a gleam of light, but how distant, how inaccessible! He was

---

17. **effaced**: wiped clean

still sinking, for the light became fainter and fainter until it was a mere glimmer. Then it began to grow and brighten, and he knew that he was rising toward the surface—knew it with reluctance, for he was now very comfortable. "To be hanged and drowned," he thought, "that is not so bad; but I do not wish to be shot. No; I will not be shot; that is not fair."

He was not conscious of an effort, but a sharp pain in his wrist apprised him that he was trying to free his hands. He gave the struggle his attention, as an idler might observe the feat of a juggler, without interest in the outcome. What splendid effort!—what magnificent, what superhuman strength! Ah, that was a fine endeavor! Bravo! The cord fell away; his arms parted and floated upward, the hands dimly seen on each side in the growing light. He watched them with a new interest as first one and then the other pounced upon the noose at his neck. They tore it away and thrust it fiercely aside, its undulations resembling those of a water snake. "Put it back, put it back!" He thought he shouted these words to his hands, for the undoing of the noose had been succeeded by the direst pang that he had yet experienced. His neck ached horribly; his brain was on fire, his heart, which had been fluttering faintly, gave a great leap, trying to force itself out at his mouth. His whole body was racked and wrenched with an insupportable anguish! But his disobedient hands gave no heed to the command. They beat the water vigorously with quick, downward strokes, forcing him to the surface. He felt his head emerge; his eyes were blinded by the sunlight; his chest expanded convulsively, and with a supreme and crowning agony his lungs engulfed a great draught of air, which instantly he expelled in a shriek!

He was now in full possession of his physical senses. They

were, indeed, preternaturally[18] keen and alert. Something in the awful disturbance of his organic system had so exalted and refined them that they made record of things never before perceived. He felt the ripples upon his face and heard their separate sounds as they struck. He looked at the forest on the bank of the stream, saw the individual trees, the leaves and the veining of each leaf—he saw the very insects upon them: the locusts,[19] the brilliant bodied flies, the gray spiders stretching their webs from twig to twig. He noted the prismatic colors in all the dewdrops upon a million blades of grass. The humming of the gnats[20] that danced above the eddies of the stream, the beating of the dragon flies' wings, the strokes of the water spiders' legs, like oars which had lifted their boat—all these made audible music. A fish slid along beneath his eyes and he heard the rush of its body parting the water.

He had come to the surface facing down the stream; in a moment the visible world seemed to wheel slowly round, himself the pivotal point, and he saw the bridge, the fort, the soldiers upon the bridge, the captain, the sergeant, the two privates, his executioners. They were in silhouette against the blue sky. They shouted and gesticulated, pointing at him. The captain had drawn his pistol, but did not fire; the others were unarmed. Their movements were grotesque and horrible, their forms gigantic.

Suddenly he heard a sharp report[21] and something struck the water smartly within a few inches of his head, spattering his face with spray. He heard a second report, and saw one of the senti-

---

18. **preternaturally**: supernaturally; out of the ordinary
19. **locust**: grasshopper
20. **gnat**: a small biting fly
21. **report**: a loud noise from a gun

nels with his rifle at his shoulder, a light cloud of blue smoke rising from the muzzle. The man in the water saw the eye of the man on the bridge gazing into his own through the sights of the rifle. He observed that it was a gray eye and remembered having read that gray eyes were keenest, and that all famous marksmen had them. Nevertheless, this one had missed.

A counter-swirl had caught Fahrquhar and turned him half round; he was again looking at the forest on the bank opposite the fort. The sound of a clear, high voice in a monotonous singsong now rang out behind him and came across the water with a distinctness that pierced and subdued all other sounds, even the beating of the ripples in his ears. Although no soldier, he had frequented camps enough to know the dread significance of that deliberate, drawling, aspirated[22] chant; the lieutenant on shore was taking a part in the morning's work. How coldly and pitilessly—with what an even, calm intonation, presaging,[23] and enforcing tranquility in the men—with what accurately measured interval fell those cruel words:

"Company!... Attention!... Shoulder arms!... Ready!... Aim!... Fire!"

Fahrquhar dived—dived as deeply as he could. The water roared in his ears like the voice of Niagara, yet he heard the dull thunder of the volley and, rising again toward the surface, met shining bits of metal, singularly flattened, oscillating[24] slowly downward. Some of them touched him on the face and hands, then fell away, continuing their descent. One lodged between his collar and neck; it was uncomfortably warm and he snatched it

---

22. **aspirated**: articulated; clear
23. **presage**: foreshadow; predict
24. **oscillate**: swing back and forth

out.

As he rose to the surface, gasping for breath, he saw that he had been a long time under water; he was perceptibly farther downstream—nearer to safety. The soldiers had almost finished reloading; the metal ramrods[25] flashed all at once in the sunshine as they were drawn from the barrels, turned in the air, and thrust into their sockets. The two sentinels fired again, independently and ineffectually.

The hunted man saw all this over his shoulder; he was now swimming vigorously with the current. His brain was as energetic as his arms and legs; he thought with the rapidity of lightning:

"The officer," he reasoned, "will not make that martinet's[26] error a second time. It is as easy to dodge a volley as a single shot. He has probably already given the command to fire at will. God help me, I cannot dodge them all!"

An appalling splash within two yards of him was followed by a loud, rushing sound, *diminuendo*,[27] which seemed to travel back through the air to the fort and died in an explosion which stirred the very river to its deeps! A rising sheet of water curved over him, fell down upon him, blinded him, strangled him! The cannon had taken a hand[28] in the game. As he shook his head free from the commotion of the smitten water he heard the deflected shot humming through the air ahead, and in an instant it was cracking and smashing the branches in the forest beyond.

---

25. **ramrod**: a rod used to pack powder and projectile into the muzzle of a gun
26. **martinet**: a strict disciplinarian in the army; the man who had his soldiers shoot all at the same time
27. **diminuendo**: decreasing in sound
28. **taken a hand**: come into play; been used

"They will not do that again," he thought; "the next time they will use a charge of grape.[29] I must keep my eye upon the gun; the smoke will apprise me—the report arrives too late; it lags behind the missile. That is a good gun."

Suddenly he felt himself whirled round and round—spinning like a top. The water, the banks, the forests, the now distant bridge, fort and men, all were commingled and blurred. Objects were represented by their colors only; circular horizontal streaks of color—that was all he saw. He had been caught in a vortex and was being whirled on with a velocity of advance and gyration that made him giddy and sick. In few moments he was flung upon the gravel at the foot of the left bank of the stream—the southern bank—and behind a projecting point which concealed him from his enemies. The sudden arrest[30] of his motion, the abrasion of one of his hands on the gravel, restored him, and he wept with delight. He dug his fingers into the sand, threw it over himself in handfuls and audibly blessed it. It looked like diamonds, rubies, emeralds; he could think of nothing beautiful which it did not resemble. The trees upon the bank were giant garden plants; he noted a definite order in their arrangement, inhaled the fragrance of their blooms. A strange roseate[31] light shone through the spaces among their trunks and the wind made in their branches the music of aeolian harps.[32] He had not wish to perfect his escape—he was content to remain in that enchanting spot until retaken.

---

29. **grape**: grapeshot; a cluster of small steel balls (resembling a cluster of grapes) used as ammunition for a cannon
30. **arrest**: stop
31. **roseate**: rose colored
32. **aeolian harp**: a harp played by the wind; said to be the instrument of Aeolus, the ancient Greek god of the winds

A whiz and a rattle of grapeshot among the branches high above his head roused him from his dream. The baffled cannoneer had fired him a random farewell. He sprang to his feet, rushed up the sloping bank, and plunged into the forest.

All that day he traveled, laying his course by the rounding sun. The forest seemed interminable;[33] nowhere did he discover a break in it, not even a woodman's road. He had not known that he lived in so wild a region. There was something uncanny in the revelation.

By nightfall he was fatigued, footsore, famished. The thought of his wife and children urged him on. At last he found a road which led him in what he knew to be the right direction. It was as wide and straight as a city street, yet it seemed untraveled. No fields bordered it, no dwelling anywhere. Not so much as the barking of a dog suggested human habitation. The black bodies of the trees formed a straight wall on both sides, terminating on the horizon in a point, like a diagram in a lesson in perspective. Overhead, as he looked up through this rift in the wood, shone great golden stars looking unfamiliar and grouped in strange constellations. He was sure they were arranged in some order which had a secret and malign significance. The wood on either side was full of singular noises, among which—once, twice, and again—he distinctly heard whispers in an unknown tongue.

His neck was in pain and lifting his hand to it found it horribly swollen. He knew that it had a circle of black where the rope had bruised it. His eyes felt congested; he could no longer close them. His tongue was swollen with thirst; he relieved its fever by thrusting it forward from between his teeth into the cold

33. interminable: unending

air. How softly the turf had carpeted the untraveled avenue—he could no longer feel the roadway beneath his feet!

Doubtless, despite his suffering, he had fallen asleep while walking, for now he sees another scene—perhaps he has merely recovered from a delirium. He stands at the gate of his own home. All is as he left it, and all bright and beautiful in the morning sunshine. He must have traveled the entire night. As he pushes open the gate and passes up the wide white walk, he sees a flutter of female garments; his wife, looking fresh and cool and sweet, steps down from the veranda to meet him. At the bottom of the steps she stands waiting, with a smile of ineffable[34] joy, an attitude of matchless grace and dignity. Ah, how beautiful she is! He springs forwards with extended arms. As he is about to clasp her he feels a stunning blow upon the back of the neck; a blinding white light blazes all about him with a sound like the shock of a cannon—then all is darkness and silence!

Peyton Fahrquhar was dead; his body, with a broken neck, swung gently from side to side beneath the timbers of the Owl Creek bridge.

---

34. **ineffable**: inexpressible

Commentary

Ambrose Bierce crafts his writing so realistically that the reader is easily drawn into the protagonist's story and is able to experience the narrative first hand. His use of character and setting in "An Occurrence at Owl Creek Bridge" combines elements of fantasy and reality—the external reality of death and the internal fantasy of Fahrquhar's escape—that breathes a life of its own. Though the story is short, Bierce divides it into three chapters to demonstrate Fahrquhar's and, to a lesser extent, the reader's erroneous beliefs.

The first chapter focuses on Fahrquhar's hanging. He is to be hung to death from the very bridge he attempted to set fire to. During the American Civil War, the Union or Federal Army, was notorious for burning plantations as they spread through the South. Fahrquhar's attempt at burning the Union bridge was his last chance to save his family and home, and join the fight against the enemy, which he was too privileged to have done in the past. Betrayed, he now is going to pay for his treachery or heroism, depending on which side of the war the reader views this travesty. The precise detail through which the hanging is described is executed with exacting military terms. There is no possible escape from his fate. The reader feels Fahrquhar is going to die; however, Fahrquhar does not. He holds onto a glimmer of hope that he can escape. Then he drops through the hole in the bridge to be hung.

The second chapter enters Fahrquhar's fantasy realm. Here is a man that is clearly not a soldier. Rich plantation owners were exempted from serving military duty; thus, ironically, the very class who wished to keep their way of life intact through slave ownership, did not have to fight in the war that would decide their very fate. Yet the proud Fahrquhar, knowing the South is losing, wishes to grab an "opportunity for distinction." He sees himself as a military hero, another fantasy. He is fooled by a Federal soldier to go to a bridge that is much more heavily guarded than he is told. He is easily captured and hung in a military fashion. In his last moments of death, he sees himself as capable of surviving his hanging, eluding gun shots from the "grey eyed" sharpshooters and the grapeshot from cannons. What Bierce has done is not only fool Fahrquhar, who has found only obscurity and death instead of heroism, but also the readers, who up until this time have read only vainglorious accounts of war, into believing that Fahrquhar has indeed escaped.

If the first and second chapter showcase Fahrquhar's disposition to fantasy, the third chapter thrusts the protagonist right into the heart of it. Fahrquhar's noose rope snaps, and he falls into a river that is incongruous. He notices "the stream racing madly beneath his feet," yet a piece of driftwood meanders at a snail's pace: "How slowly it appeared to move! What a sluggish stream!" Furthermore, the last thing he thinks of before he is hung is to "throw off the noose and spring into the stream. By diving I could evade the bullets and, swimming vigorously, reach the bank, take to the woods and get away home." When he loses consciousness, his fevered mind begins to act out the last thoughts he had. The reader may understand that Fahrquhar has passed over the threshold into a land of fancy, for he experiences the world around him in such acute detail—the vegetation, insects, and river, even the riverbank looks "like diamonds, rubies, emeralds"—that such observance is impossible for a man fleeing for his life. At the moment of his death, he even experiences the ticking of his watch as the death knell (similar to Poe's death watches), reminiscent of the poet John Donne's words about the coming certainty of death in Meditation XVII: "Therefore never send to know for whom the bell tolls; it tolls for thee."

If all these experiences have failed to alert the reader to Fahrquhar's death, his journey home should. The road he treads upon is wide as a city's yet empty of people as well as any habitation. As he walks through a forest, all is dark and full of ghostly voices, he feels pain in his swollen neck (the noose tightening), his eyes so congested he cannot close them (blood or tears filling his eyes; eyes bugging out from suffocation), and his tongue enlarged so that he has to stick it out of his mouth (tongue dangling out from lack of oxygen). He even starts to feel weightless and cannot feel the ground he walks upon, an obvious signal that poor Farquhar is hanging from the gallows and suffocating to death. Then he suddenly feels a sharp blow to his neck followed by his vision filling with white light. The noose has snapped his neck at this point and he dies, along with his flights of fantasy. Farquhar has gone from a man questing to be a war hero, a patriot of the South, to being the "the man who is engaged in being hanged."

Introduction of the Author

Edgar Allan Poe (1809-1849)

Judged to be the father of the detective story and of modern horror, Edgar Allan Poe was born January 19, 1809, the son of two poor traveling theater actors; a profession that was not all that esteemed at the time. Edgar's father, David Poe, often appeared drunk on stage and was a notorious drinker and even abandoned his family when Edgar was two years old. A year later his mother died violently of tuberculosis, an event that traumatized him into his later years. Edgar was then taken in by the Allans, though never legally adopted, and given the best education, which included five years in England. Poe entered the University of Virginia where he dropped out a year later after falling into debt due to gambling. His year-long engagement to Sarah Elmira Royster soon fell apart, and he also had a falling away with the Allans. Facing a dismal, penniless future, Poe enlisted in the army in 1827, and even wrote poems. His first book of poetry appeared in *Tamerlane and Other Poems*, a style that borrowed heavily from the English poet Lord Byron.

To more or less appease his foster father, John Allan, Poe entered the army at West Point, a top military academy, to be an officer. When John Allan remarried, his new wife refused to be Poe's mother. After being disowned by the Allans, Poe quit West Point by intentionally disobeying orders and receiving a court martial. To avoid going to military prison, he gladly accepted dismissal from West point and turned to writing full time as a contributor to several magazines from 1835 to 1843. Thus, he became the first American writer to make a living on publishing alone. During this time, he published some of his best known stories. He moved to Baltimore and lived with his widowed Aunt and her daughter, Virginia Clem. Poe was the center of several scandals when his drinking became well known. He also caused a stir when he married his 13 year old cousin, Virginia, who died of tuberculosis five years after bursting a blood vessel and becoming an invalid. The drinking nearly destroyed him after the death of his wife. Poe still maintained legitimacy as a writer, as an adept literary critic, and by publishing "The Murders in the Rue Morgue" (1841), which became the precursor to the great works of mystery that followed, especially Sir Arthur Conan Doyle's Sherlock Holmes character. He also is argued as being the creator of the short story form, though this is still much in debate; one of his most famous short stories being the Gothic fiction "A Tell-Tale Heart" (1843).

By 1845, Poe had moved to New York where he penned his now famous poem "The Raven." His erratic behavior and bouts of madness led to many rumors, many now proven false. His critics labeled him a drug addict, while others said he attempted suicide by overdosing on the drug laudanum. Many of these speculations have since been proven false. Since Poe became associated with tales of the macabre and was well known for being an alcoholic, many thought the dark characters of his stories as being somewhat autobiographical. After years of such physical and mental abuse—the death of his wife, and abject poverty—Poe was found unconscious in the gutter on October 3, 1849. He stayed in this state for four more days before he died. The rumor mill has since said he was murdered, suffered from disease, or died of alcoholism. However he passed away, the literary world now recognizes a lost genius to the fiction genre.

The Tell-Tale Heart

TRUE!—nervous—very, very dreadfully nervous I had been and am; but why *will* you say that I am mad? The disease had sharpened my senses—not destroyed—not dulled them. Above all was the sense of hearing acute.[1] I heard all things in the heaven and in the earth. I heard many things in hell. How, then, am I mad? Hearken! and observe how healthily—how calmly I can tell you the whole story.

It is impossible to say how first the idea entered my brain; but once conceived, it haunted me day and night. Object there was none. Passion there was none. I loved the old man. He had never wronged me. He had never given me insult. For his gold I had no desire. I think it was his eye! yes, it was this! He had the eye of a vulture—a pale blue eye, with a film over it. Whenever it fell upon me, my blood ran cold; and so by degrees—very gradually—I made up my mind to take the life of the old man, and thus rid myself of the eye forever.

Now this is the point. You fancy me mad. Madmen know nothing. But you should have seen *me*. You should have seen how wisely I proceeded—with what caution—with what foresight—with what dissimulation[2] I went to work! I was never kinder to the old man than during the whole week before I killed him. And every night, about midnight, I turned the latch of his door and opened it—oh so gently! And then, when I had made an

---

1. **acute**: highly sensitive
2. **dissimulation**: concealment

opening sufficient for my head, I put in a dark lantern, all closed, closed, so that no light shone out, and then I thrust in my head. Oh, you would have laughed to see how cunningly I thrust it in! I moved it slowly—very, very slowly, so that I might not disturb the old man's sleep. It took me an hour to place my whole head within the opening so far that I could see him as he lay upon his bed. Ha!—would a madman have been so wise as this? And then, when my head was well in the room, I undid the lantern cautiously—oh, so cautiously—cautiously (for the hinges creaked)—I undid it just so much that a single thin ray fell upon the vulture eye. And this I did for seven long nights—every night just at midnight—but I found the eye always closed; and so it was impossible to do the work; for it was not the old man who vexed[3] me, but his Evil Eye. And every morning, when the day broke, I went boldly into the chamber, and spoke courageously to him, calling him by name in a hearty tone, and inquiring how he has passed the night. So you see he would have been a very profound[4] old man, indeed, to suspect that every night, just at twelve, I looked in upon him while he slept.

Upon the eighth night I was more than usually cautious in opening the door. A watch's minute hand moves more quickly than did mine. Never before that night had I *felt* the extent of my own powers—of my sagacity.[5] I could scarcely contain my feelings of triumph. To think that there I was, opening the door, little by little, and he not even to dream of my secret deeds or thoughts. I fairly chuckled at the idea; and perhaps he heard me; for he moved on the bed suddenly, as if startled. Now you may

3. **vexed**: annoyed
4. **profound**: deeply thinking
5. **sagacity**: wisdom

think that I drew back—but no. His room was as black as pitch[6] with the thick darkness, (for the shutters were close fastened, through fear of robbers,) and so I knew that he could not see the opening of the door, and I kept pushing it on steadily, steadily.

I had my head in, and was about to open the lantern, when my thumb slipped upon the tin fastening, and the old man sprang up in bed, crying out—"Who's there?"

I kept quite still and said nothing. For a whole hour I did not move a muscle, and in the meantime I did not hear him lie down. He was still sitting up in the bed listening;—just as I have done, night after night, hearkening to the death watches[7] in the wall.

Presently I heard a slight groan, and I knew it was the groan of mortal terror. It was not a groan of pain or of grief—oh, no!—it was the low stifled sound that arises from the bottom of the soul when overcharged with awe. I knew the sound well. Many a night, just at midnight, when all the world slept, it has welled up from my own bosom, deepening, with its dreadful echo, the terrors that distracted me. I say I knew it well. I knew what the old man felt, and pitied him, although I chuckled at heart. I knew that he had been lying awake ever since the first slight noise, when he had turned in the bed. His fears had been ever since growing upon him. He had been trying to fancy them causeless, but could not. He had been saying to himself—"It is nothing but the wind in the chimney—it is only a mouse crossing the floor," or "It is merely a cricket which has made a single

---

6. **pitch**: tar

7. **death watches**: insects that nested in walls and made sounds similar to ticking clocks

chirp." Yes, he had been trying to comfort himself with these suppositions:[8] but he had found all in vain. *All in vain;* because Death, in approaching him had stalked with his black shadow before him, and enveloped the victim. And it was the mournful influence of the unperceived shadow that caused him to feel—although he neither saw nor heard—to *feel* the presence of my head within the room.

When I had waited a long time, very patiently, without hearing him lie down, I resolved to open a little—a very, very little crevice in the lantern. So I opened it—you cannot imagine how stealthily, stealthily—until, at length a single dim ray, like the thread of the spider, shot from out the crevice and fell full upon the vulture eye.

It was open—wide, wide open—and I grew furious as I gazed upon it. I saw it with perfect distinctness—all a dull blue, with a hideous veil over it that chilled the very marrow in my bones; but I could see nothing else of the old man's face or person: for I had directed the ray as if by instinct, precisely upon the damned spot.

And have I not told you that what you mistake for madness is but over acuteness[9] of the senses?—now, I say, there came to my ears a low, dull, quick sound, such as a watch makes when enveloped in cotton. I knew *that* sound well, too. It was the beating of the old man's heart. It increased my fury, as the beating of a drum stimulates the soldier into courage.

But even yet I refrained and kept still. I scarcely breathed. I held the lantern motionless. I tried how steadily I could maintain the ray upon the eye. Meantime the hellish tattoo of the heart

---

8. **suppositions**: assumptions

9. **acuteness**: sensitivity

increased. It grew quicker and quicker, and louder and louder every instant. The old man's terror *must* have been extreme! It grew louder, I say, louder every moment!—do you mark me well? I have told you that I am nervous: so I am. And now at the dead hour of the night, amid the dreadful silence of that old house, so strange a noise as this excited me to uncontrollable terror. Yet, for some minutes longer I refrained and stood still. But the beating grew louder, louder! I thought the heart must burst. And now a new anxiety seized me—the sound would be heard by a neighbor! The old man's hour had come! With a loud yell, I threw open the lantern and leaped into the room. He shrieked once—once only. In an instant I dragged him to the floor, and pulled the heavy bed over him. I then smiled gaily, to find the deed so far done. But, for many minutes, the heart beat on with a muffled sound. This, however, did not vex me; it would not be heard through the wall. At length it ceased. The old man was dead. I removed the bed and examined the corpse. Yes, he was stone, stone dead. I placed my hand upon the heart and held it there many minutes. There was no pulsation. He was stone dead. His eye would trouble me no more.

If still you think me mad, you will think so no longer when I describe the wise precautions I took for the concealment of the body. The night waned,[10] and I worked hastily, but in silence. First of all I dismembered the corpse. I cut off the head and the arms and the legs.

I then took up three planks from the flooring of the chamber, and deposited all between the scantlings. I then replaced the boards so cleverly, so cunningly, that no human eye—not even *his*—could have detected any thing wrong. There was nothing to

---

10. **waned**: came to an end

wash out—no stain of any kind—no blood-spot whatever. I had been too wary for that. A tub had caught all—ha! ha!

When I had made an end of these labors, it was four o'clock —still dark as midnight. As the bell sounded the hour, there came a knocking at the street door. I went down to open it with a light heart,—for what had I now to fear? There entered three men, who introduced themselves, with perfect suavity,[11] as officers of the police. A shriek had been heard by a neighbor during the night; suspicion of foul play had been aroused; information had been lodged at the police office, and they (the officers) had been deputed to search the premises.

I smiled,—for *what* had I to fear? I bade the gentlemen welcome. The shriek, I said, was my own in a dream. The old man, I mentioned, was absent in the country. I took my visitors all over the house. I bade them search—search well. I led them, at length, to *his* chamber. I showed them his treasures, secure, undisturbed. In the enthusiasm of my confidence, I brought chairs into the room, and desired them *here* to rest from their fatigues, while I myself, in the wild audacity[12] of my perfect triumph, placed my own seat upon the very spot beneath which reposed the corpse of the victim.

The officers were satisfied. My *manner* had convinced them. I was singularly at ease. They sat, and while I answered cheerily, they chatted of familiar things. But, ere long, I felt myself getting pale and wished them gone. My head ached, and I fancied a ringing in my ears: but still they sat and still chatted. The ringing became more distinct:—it continued and became more distinct: I talked more freely to get rid of the feeling: but it continued and

---

11. **suavity**: courtesy
12. **audacity**: confidence or boldness

gained definiteness—until, at length, I found that the noise was *not* within my ears.

No doubt I now grew very pale;—but I talked more fluently, and with a heightened voice. Yet the sound increased—and what could I do? It was *a low, dull, quick sound—much such a sound as a watch makes when enveloped in cotton.*

I gasped for breath—and yet the officers heard it not. I talked more quickly—more vehemently;[13] but the noise steadily increased. I arose and argued about trifles, in a high key and with violent gesticulations;[14] but the noise steadily increased. Why *would* they not be gone? I paced the floor to and fro with heavy strides, as if excited to fury by the observations of the men —but the noise steadily increased. Oh God! what *could* I do? I foamed—I raved—I swore! I swung the chair upon which I had been sitting, and grated it upon the boards, but the noise arose over all and continually increased. It grew louder—louder—*louder!* And still the men chatted pleasantly, and smiled. Was it possible they heard not? Almighty God!—no, no! They heard!—they suspected!—they knew!—they were making a mockery of my horror! —this I thought, and this I think. But anything was better than this agony! Anything was more tolerable than this derision! I could bear those hypocritical smiles no longer! I felt that I must scream or die!—and now—again!—hark! louder! louder! louder! *louder*!—

"Villains!" I shrieked, "dissemble[15] no more! I admit the deed!—tear up the planks!—here, here!—it is the beating of his hideous heart!"

---

13. **vehemently**: intensely
14. **gesticulations**: movements
15. **dissemble**: hide true thoughts

Commentary

Edgar Allan Poe's "A Tell-Tale Heart" is a prime example of Gothic fiction, a mixture of horror and romance. Horror grew out of the Romantic Movement, for it was the goal of Romantic writers to deal with topics and ideas that were not ordinary. Horror attempts to unsettle the reader by combining the ideals established in the Romantic Movement of presenting situations that most readers had never encountered. Gothic fiction often takes place in dark, austere buildings rooted in Gothic architecture similar to medieval castles and Roman Catholic cathedrals. The villainous and monstrous protagonists of Gothic fiction are usually as severe as the architecture itself, creating moral ambiguity that often shocked the nineteenth century sensibilities. Poe became the master of Gothic fiction because he felt that the ordinary could be experienced at any point in time; thus, the notable events should be the focus of fiction.

The narrator, being the stereotypical Gothic villain and madman (or is it a woman?), attempts to convince the reader that he is not mad. It is interesting to note that he never tries to persuade the reader that he is not guilty of murder, only that he is not mad. His attempts at rationality only prove he is more irrational. The narrator seems to be vigorously explaining his frame of mind to the very police that have come knocking at his door at the end of the story. He is obviously guilty after his confession. The police probably have a shocked expression on their faces, and with revulsion spit out, "Are you mad?!!" To which the narrator replies at the beginning of the story: "Why *will* you say that I am mad?" He wishes the police to know that he is suffering from nervousness and not madness. Here Poe redefines what Gothic literature should be. In the past, the norm was to have actual monsters (vampires, ghosts, Frankenstein's monster) create the horror, where the protagonists suffered under the weight of nervousness and fear of death from the hands of these creatures. Poe created terror coming not from without but from within—the soul. Moreover, this narrator is someone far more terrifying than a vampire or golem; he is human, a person you may work with, live with, share your life with. This is the reason the narrator of this story, as in most of Poe's stories, is nameless. His tormentor and victim is the actual monster with the "eye of a vulture—a pale blue eye, with a film over it." Yet humans prove to be far more monstrous in stamping out creatures and ideas that they do not understand.

What Poe clearly says in this story is that the physical appearance is not what makes a person beastly but the actions. The narrator demonstrates predator psychology as he premeditates and plans his attack like a lion circling its prey, wearing it down. He first stays out of sight, so the old man never suspects; he stalks him at night and offers a crocodile's smile in the morning. Then on the eighth night, he pounces! The terror a lion's prey must feel is the same that the victim in this tale feels when the narrator accidentally makes a noise and alerts the old man, who sits up calling out in fear. The narrator takes joy in the situation: "Presently I heard a slight groan, and I knew it was the groan of mortal terror... I chuckled at heart." He uses his cool, analytical demeanor to reassure the reader that he is not mad, for what madman could so calmly carry out the sort of murder he has committed, to which the reader would respond, "a madman!" It is his own blindness to his condition that horrifies the reader and the old man. He almost feels right in what he does. He brags about how he prepares for seven nights to enter the old man's room, how still he would wait, poking his head through the crack in the door and testing his own endurance of stillness. He is a phantom in the shadows, a vampire hovering over the bed, the ghost in the attic, and yet he is the most trusted person in the old man's house. The horror!

What also adds to the Gothic element of this tale is Poe's attention to atmosphere: the dark rooms, lanterns with creaky hinges, windows securely shuddered, and rooms devoid of any light. Even the overall location of the tale creates a mysterious ambiance. The reader has no clue as to where the country, city, or even the type of house this tale takes place in, which was, for Poe, an essential element of Romantic literature. Even the death watches in the wall add to the overwhelming dread that this dark house encapsulates, for to hear them was to hear doom approach. These insects take the place of the rustic grandfather clock ticking in the corner, reminding the reader that fear is not mechanical or false, but natural and alive. The sounds of these bugs are soon replaced with the more repetitive and consistent beating of the human heart.

Here is another convention of romantic literature turned into horror. The heart is a natural part of life that sustains all through its incessant beating and is often associated with love and compassion. Here Poe effectively uses it against the narrator as a form of terror that will undo him in the end. The beating of the old man's heart, first, drives the narrator to new anger beyond what the fiendish eye had done. "It was the beating of the old man's heart. It increased my fury." Little does the narrator realize that the beating heart is not the old man's but his own, created from his own guilt. A sound that he hears even after the old man is dead. The tell-tale sound of his own guilty heart beating is the sound that drives him further and further into madness until he must confess his crimes to the police. While the narrator ultimately does suffer under the malady of nervousness, it is his own madness that undoes him; his madness is the very monster that drives his nerves to fray and ultimately destroys him.

British Short Stories

Oscar Wilde: The Sphinx without a Secret (1891)
Saki: The Open Window (1914)
James Joyce: A Painful Case (1914)
Virginia Woolf: The Mark on the Wall (1921)
H. G. Wells: The Remarkable Case of Davidson's Eyes (1895)

Introduction of the Author

Oscar Wilde *(1854-1900)*

Though Oscar Wilde lived his later life in controversy and even suffered arrest, he has since been redeemed as an original poet, one of the greatest playwrights of the Victorian Age, and an influence on the youth through his fairy tales. Oscar was born Fingal O'Flahertie Wills Wilde on October 16, 1854 in Dublin, Ireland. His philanthropist father, Sir William Wilde, opened his medical clinic for ear and eye disease to the poor and needy, and his well educated mother, Francesca Wilde, was a journalist and a poet who wrote her poetry under the pseudonym, "Speranza." Oscar was home schooled as a child and later went on to graduate from Trinity College, Dublin. While in college his prowess with words surfaced, and he won various awards and scholarships for his works, especially poetry. He fell in love with Florence Balcome, who later got engaged to Bram Stoker, of later *Dracula* fame. The loss of his love was one of the causes for Wilde to leave Ireland and start on a successful career as a traveling lecturer in America, London, and Paris from 1881 to 1882.

In 1884, Wilde married Constance Lloyd, an educated woman, and had two children in succession the following two years. Perhaps forced to make a living for his family, Wilde's greatest efforts followed for the next six years. In 1888, he published a collection of children's fairy tales *The Happy Prince and Other Tales*. His only novel, *The Picture of Dorian Gray* (1891), was published a year earlier in short story form for an American magazine and was met with critical disappointment, though it is considered a classic now. *Lord Arthur Savile's Crime and Other Stories*, his next collection of short stories published in 1891, was remarkable in that it satirizes America's social simplicity along with Britain's aristocratic pretentiousness. Though Gothic fiction was in vogue, he particularly satirized its literary conventions. The collection contained the short story "A Sphinx without a Secret," which satirizes Victorian views of woman, and the effects such views have. He followed this with a second collection of children's stories, *The House of Pomegranates* (1892). Though he did publish collections of poetry, Wilde is most famous as a dramatist, his most popular being the very witty *The Importance of Being Earnest* (1895).

Wilde was a man well ahead of his time, for neither the Victorians nor the Americans wanted anything to do with him. In a style that is considered fashionable and even masculine today, Wilde started to wear his hair long and became overly concerned about appearance and thought sports unintelligent. He embraced aestheticism, which carried the slogan "art for art's sake," and many blasted him as being decadent. The main reason is that the Aesthetic Movement pushed for pleasure of the senses over moral messages, so, instead of literature providing instruction on life, it should just be beautiful because it can be. This included not only what they wrote but how they lived as well; thus, life should imitate art. And Oscar Wilde imitated it to the utmost. In a style that would be considered metrosexual in today's modern society, Wilde decorated his rooms with peacock feathers, flowers, expensive china, and art. His manner of dress and action resulted in suffering the humiliation of a public dunking in the River Cherwell. Though his children's fairy tales were quite didactic, his novels and short stories were famously aesthetic.

However, out of all his success, Wilde's carefree lifestyle in the conservative Victorian Age was his downfall. First hinted at when he wrote of Shakespeare's famous sonnets being addressed to a boy, Wilde's own sexuality became a scandal as well. Wilde began to have a sexual relationship with a young fan, a seventeen year old boy at the time, which set the boy's father off in a rage. The father publicly slandered Wilde, whereupon Wilde sued. The truth of Wilde's homosexuality was eventually brought out in the trial, and Wilde was arrested for what was then known as "gross indecency." He was subjected to two years of hard labor, which ruined his health. Upon his release, he changed his name and wrote under the pen names of Sebastian Melmoth and C. 3. 3. He lived the rest of his life in poverty, when, three years later, he died of cerebral meningitis in Paris on November 30, 1900. Wilde may have died in shame, but his work and genius live on as adults and children alike read and respect his works as true classics.

The Sphinx without a Secret

One afternoon I was sitting outside the Café de la Paix,[1] watching the splendour and shabbiness of Parisian life, and wondering over my vermouth[2] at the strange panorama of pride and poverty that was passing before me, when I heard some one call my name. I turned round, and saw Lord Murchison. We had not met since we had been at college together, nearly ten years before, so I was delighted to come across him again, and we shook hands warmly. At Oxford we had been great friends. I had liked him immensely, he was so handsome, so high-spirited, and so honourable. We used to say of him that he would be the best of fellows, if he did not always speak the truth, but I think we really admired him all the more for his frankness. I found him a good deal changed. He looked anxious and puzzled, and seemed to be in doubt about something. I felt it could not be modern scepticism, for Murchison was the stoutest of Tories,[3] and believed in the Pentateuch[4] as firmly as he believed in the House of Peers;[5] so I concluded that it was a woman, and asked him if he was married yet.

---

1. **Café de la Paix**: a famous café located in northern district of Paris, France, where, it is said, one is bound to always meet an acquaintance since the site is so popular
2. **vermouth**: a white wine flavored with a variety of herbs and roots
3. **Tory**: a member of the British conservative political party
4. **Pentateuch**: the first five books of the Old Testament: Genesis, Exodus, Leviticus, Numbers, and Deuteronomy
5. **House of Peers**: a personal reference to the British House of Lords, the upper house of Parliament

'I don't understand women well enough,' he answered.

'My dear Gerald,' I said, 'women are meant to be loved, not to be understood.'

'I cannot love where I cannot trust,' he replied.

'I believe you have a mystery in your life, Gerald,' I exclaimed; 'tell me about it.'

'Let us go for a drive,' he answered, 'it is too crowded here. No, not a yellow carriage, any other colour—there, that dark green one will do'; and in a few moments we were trotting down the boulevard in the direction of the Madeleine.[6]

'Where shall we go to?' I said.

'Oh, anywhere you like!' he answered—'to the restaurant in the Bois;[7] we will dine there, and you shall tell me all about yourself.'

'I want to hear about you first,' I said. 'Tell me your mystery.'

He took from his pocket a little silver-clasped morocco[8] case, and handed it to me. I opened it. Inside there was the photograph of a woman. She was tall and slight, and strangely picturesque with her large vague eyes and loosened hair. She looked like a clairvoyante,[9] and was wrapped in rich furs.

'What do you think of that face?' he said; 'is it truthful?'

I examined it carefully. It seemed to me the face of some one who had a secret, but whether that secret was good or evil I could not say. Its beauty was a beauty moulded out of many

---

6. **Madeleine**: a Catholic church originally designed as a temple to glorify Napoleon's army
7. **Bois**: a park in Paris to the southeast of the character's current location
8. **morocco**: a dark red colored goatskin leather
9. **clairvoyante**: French spelling of clairvoyant, a person who can see beyond normal vision; a fortune teller

mysteries—the beauty, in fact, which is psychological, not plastic —and the faint smile that just played across the lips was far too subtle to be really sweet.

'Well,' he cried impatiently, 'what do you say?'

'She is the Gioconda[10] in sables,[11]' I answered. 'Let me know all about her.'

'Not now,' he said; 'after dinner,' and began to talk of other things.

When the waiter brought us our coffee and cigarettes I reminded Gerald of his promise. He rose from his seat, walked two or three times up and down the room, and, sinking into an armchair, told me the following story: —

'One evening,' he said, 'I was walking down Bond Street[12] about five o'clock. There was a terrific crush of carriages, and the traffic was almost stopped. Close to the pavement was standing a little yellow brougham,[13] which, for some reason or other, attracted my attention. As I passed by there looked out from it the face I showed you this afternoon. It fascinated me immediately. All that night I kept thinking of it, and all the next day. I wandered up and down that wretched Row,[14] peering into every carriage, and waiting for the yellow brougham; but I could not find *ma belle inconnue*,[15] and at last I began to think she was merely a dream. About a week afterwards I was dining with Madame de Rastail. Dinner was for eight o'clock; but at half-past eight

---

10. **Gioconda**: the Italian name of the Mona Lisa by Leonardo da Vinci
11. **sables**: furs made of martins, weasel like creatures
12. **Bond Street**: a major street in London, England
13. **brougham**: a small horse-drawn carriage
14. **Row**: a small English street
15. ***ma belle inconnue***: French for "my lovely unknown woman"

we were still waiting in the drawing-room. Finally the servant threw open the door, and announced Lady Alroy. It was the woman I had been looking for. She came in very slowly, looking like a moonbeam in grey lace, and, to my intense delight, I was asked to take her in to dinner. After we had sat down, I remarked quite innocently, "I think I caught sight of you in Bond Street some time ago, Lady Alroy." She grew very pale, and said to me in a low voice, "Pray do not talk so loud; you may be overheard." I felt miserable at having made such a bad beginning, and plunged recklessly into the subject of the French plays. She spoke very little, always in the same low musical voice, and seemed as if she was afraid of some one listening. I fell passionately, stupidly in love, and the indefinable atmosphere of mystery that surrounded her excited my most ardent[16] curiosity. When she was going away, which she did very soon after dinner, I asked her if I might call and see her. She hesitated for a moment, glanced round to see if any one was near us, and then said, "Yes; to-morrow at a quarter to five." I begged Madame de Rastail to tell me about her; but all that I could learn was that she was a widow with a beautiful house in Park Lane,[17] and as some scientific bore began a dissertation on widows, as exemplifying the survival of the matrimonially fittest, I left and went home.

'The next day I arrived at Park Lane punctual to the moment, but was told by the butler that Lady Alroy had just gone out. I went down to the club quite unhappy and very much puzzled, and after long consideration wrote her a letter, asking if I might be allowed to try my chance some other afternoon. I had no answer for several days, but at last I got a little note saying

---

16. **ardent**: passionate

17. **Park Lane**: a major road in central London

she would be at home on Sunday at four and with this extraordinary postscript: "Please do not write to me here again; I will explain when I see you." On Sunday she received me, and was perfectly charming; but when I was going away she begged of me, if I ever had occasion to write to her again, to address my letter to "Mrs. Knox, care of Whittaker's Library, Green Street." "There are reasons," she said, "why I cannot receive letters in my own house."

'All through the season I saw a great deal of her, and the atmosphere of mystery never left her. Sometimes I thought that she was in the power of some man, but she looked so unapproachable, that I could not believe it. It was really very difficult for me to come to any conclusion, for she was like one of those strange crystals that one sees in museums, which are at one moment clear, and at another clouded. At last I determined to ask her to be my wife: I was sick and tired of the incessant[18] secrecy that she imposed on all my visits, and on the few letters I sent her. I wrote to her at the library to ask her if she could see me the following Monday at six. She answered yes, and I was in the seventh heaven[19] of delight. I was infatuated with her: in spite of the mystery, I thought then—in consequence of it, I see now. No; it was the woman herself I loved. The mystery troubled me, maddened me. Why did chance put me in its track?'

'You discovered it, then?' I cried.

'I fear so,' he answered. 'You can judge for yourself.'

'When Monday came round I went to lunch with my uncle,

---

18. **incessant**: unending
19. **seventh heaven**: according to Semitic religions the cosmos is divided into seven heavens with the seventh being the greatest and reserved for the purest souls

and about four o'clock found myself in the Marylebone Road.[20] My uncle, you know, lives in Regent's Park.[21] I wanted to get to Piccadilly, and took a short cut through a lot of shabby little streets. Suddenly I saw in front of me Lady Alroy, deeply veiled and walking very fast. On coming to the last house in the street, she went up the steps, took out a latch-key, and let herself in. "Here is the mystery," I said to myself; and I hurried on and examined the house. It seemed a sort of place for letting lodgings. On the doorstep lay her handkerchief, which she had dropped. I picked it up and put it in my pocket. Then I began to consider what I should do. I came to the conclusion that I had no right to spy on her, and I drove down to the club. At six I called to see her. She was lying on a sofa, in a tea-gown of silver tissue looped up by some strange moonstones that she always wore. She was looking quite lovely. "I am so glad to see you," she said; "I have not been out all day." I stared at her in amazement, and pulling the handkerchief out of my pocket, handed it to her. "You dropped this in Cumnor Street this afternoon, Lady Alroy," I said very calmly. She looked at me in terror but made no attempt to take the handkerchief. "What were you doing there?" I asked. "What right have you to question me?" she answered. "The right of a man who loves you," I replied; "I came here to ask you to be my wife." She hid her face in her hands, and burst into floods of tears. "You must tell me," I continued. She stood up, and, looking me straight in the face, said, "Lord Murchison, there is nothing to tell you."—"You went to meet some one," I cried; "this is your mystery." She grew dreadfully white, and

20. **Marylebone Road**: a major bypass in central London

21. **Regent's Park**: A royal park in northern central London that was originally commissioned by King George IV

said, "I went to meet no one."—"Can't you tell the truth?" I exclaimed. "I have told it," she replied. I was mad, frantic; I don't know what I said, but I said terrible things to her. Finally I rushed out of the house. She wrote me a letter the next day; I sent it back unopened, and started for Norway with Alan Colville. After a month I came back, and the first thing I saw in the Morning Post was the death of Lady Alroy. She had caught a chill at the Opera, and had died in five days of congestion of the lungs. I shut myself up and saw no one. I had loved her so much, I had loved her so madly. Good God! how I had loved that woman!'

'You went to the street, to the house in it?' I said.

'Yes,' he answered.

'One day I went to Cumnor Street. I could not help it; I was tortured with doubt. I knocked at the door, and a respectable-looking woman opened it to me. I asked her if she had any rooms to let.[22] "Well, sir," she replied, "the drawing-rooms are supposed to be let; but I have not seen the lady for three months, and as rent is owing on them, you can have them."—"Is this the lady?" I said, showing the photograph. "That's her, sure enough," she exclaimed; "and when is she coming back, sir?"—"The lady is dead," I replied. "Oh sir, I hope not!" said the woman; "she was my best lodger. She paid me three guineas[23] a week merely to sit in my drawing-rooms now and then." "She met some one here?" I said; but the woman assured me that it was not so, that she always came alone, and saw no one. "What on earth did she do here?" I cried. "She simply sat in the draw-

---

22. **let**: rent

23. **guineas**: gold coin currency used in the United Kingdom that later meant 21 shillings (£1.05)

ing-room, sir, reading books, and sometimes had tea," the woman answered. I did not know what to say, so I gave her a sovereign[24] and went away. Now, what do you think it all meant? You don't believe the woman was telling the truth?'

'I do.'

'Then why did Lady Alroy go there?'

'My dear Gerald,' I answered, 'Lady Alroy was simply a woman with a mania for mystery. She took these rooms for the pleasure of going there with her veil down, and imagining she was a heroine. She had a passion for secrecy, but she herself was merely a Sphinx without a secret.'

'Do you really think so?'

'I am sure of it,' I replied.

He took out the morocco case, opened it, and looked at the photograph. 'I wonder?' he said at last.

---

24. **sovereign**: a British coin still in use worth 20 shillings

Commentary

Oscar Wilde's "The Sphinx without a Secret" is the type of story scholars and critics eschew for its simplicity and self explanatory title that seems to deflate the climax of the story. However, Oscar Wilde was no hack of a writer, and what he wrote had a purpose. As a leading member of the Aesthetic Movement, Wilde's main purpose of writing was to separate art from morality, and he veiwed the didactic, as Edgar Allan Poe did, as a heresy of story writing. "Art for art's sake" became the motto of the practicing aesthetic, whose main concern was how art was perceived and recognized. In order to appreciate just what Oscar Wilde is trying to show in this short story, an understanding of how he viewed women and art is necessary.

Wilde, as most aesthetics, saw the human form as a work of art and that life should imitate art. This translates to the feminine as well. In most of Wilde's fiction, he satirized Victorian men's view of women as passive works of art that should be seen instead of heard. In *The Picture of Dorian Gray* (1890), the Duchess asks Lord Henry, Dorian's cousin, to describe the female sex; he replies they are "sphinxes without secrets." A prior comment that sparks this question is her own reference to herself, and women in general being like Icarus, flying close to the sun, but never burning her wings. In her own mind, she sees herself as daring and adventurous in pursuing the attentions of Dorian Gray. Lord Henry, however, retorts that she uses her wings for everything except flight, hinting that she does not have any daring or sense of adventure, and she will most surly lose to another woman bolder in her pursuit of Dorian's love. In other words, Victorian men view women as grounded peacocks showing off their plume, but never amounting to any sort of flight.

However, Wilde writes in his stage play *An Ideal Husband* that the butler is similar to a sphinx that "is not incommunicable. He is a mask with a manner. Of his intellectual or emotional life, history knows nothing. He represents the dominance of form." Sphinxes are meant to communicate. They have the mask of decorum that hides their true identity. They are works of art in and of themselves, and their "dominance of form" is what people fear. Translate this into "The Sphinx without a Secret." The woman Lady Alroy is spoken of from a male perspective. The narrator never has a chance to see this woman first hand. All he has to go on is a photograph of her. The woman is given no voice. This is why the sphinx has no secret—she has no voice to tell her secret with. The sphinx of ancient Greece, which Wilde most likely referenced, sat on a precipice and asked riddles to the unwary. When the riddle could not be answered, the victim was either devoured or hurtled off the cliff. If the riddle was, by some chance, answered correctly, the sphinx, in a state of dismay, would thrash around and hurl itself off the cliff to its death. Yet, how is the sphinx supposed to function without a voice? Art and male portrayals of women have reduced them to figures and not people. Lady Alroy has no way to express her interest in mystery, which is dominated by males, or function in a social society, also dominated by males, in a Victorian England. All she has are her books and her own personal air of mystery. When Lord Murchison interprets her actions as real (he thinks she is having an affair with another man) he abandons her. He has solved her riddle incorrectly, and, ironically, instead of being devoured by the sphinx, it is the sphinx that is doomed to die.

Finally, Wilde views Victorian women as being confused as to their own identity, which is given to them by the dominant male society. Lady Alroy, assuming Lord Murchison and other men love an air of mystery about a woman, goes out of her way to create one, yet her secret is her own affection for secrets and her need to appear mysterious to attract a man. She turns out to be a just a book worm, a woman desperately trying to capture a man, a sphinx without a secret, which, in reality, is not very attractive at all. Yet, Lord Murchison seems to have learned his lesson. Notice it is only the narrator's point of view of Lady Alroy near the end of the story, and not Murchison's. This is the reason the story ends with, "I wonder." Lord Murchison's point of view is shifting. He is not willing to accept that she has no secret, for she does. Why else would a beautiful, respectable "Lady" go around pretending to have a mystery in her life in order to capture the hearts of men?

Introduction of the Author

Saki *(1870-1916)*

Hector Hugh Munro, famously known by his pen name Saki, was born in Burma (present day Myanmar) at the height of the Victorian period (1837-1901), which was a period of great prosperity and the peak of the British Empire. His father was the chief inspector for the Burma police. The Munros soon moved back to England, where his father left him, his mother, and his two siblings in care of two aunts before he left for India. Munro's mother was killed by a stampeding cow when he was two. His strict aunts raised him, and he received a good education. His father only visited once a year, and his childhood was overseen by women who were far from maternal. His father liked to travel, so he saw France, Germany, and Switzerland during his adolescence. Though his father eventually settled back down in England to be a teacher, Munro returned to Burma to join the Burma police when he was 23. Having enough adventure for three years, he was never a healthy boy and suffered from malaria, he returned to England to be a journalist.

Munro's writing career started in 1900 with the publication of his first book, *The Rise of the Russian Empire*, a historical study that attempted to document the Russian Empire as Edward Gibbon successfully did for the Romans in *The Decline and Fall of the Roman Empire* (1788). Munro's work failed to inspire as its predecessor did, and was even ridiculed in America. Luckily, Munro still had his day job, and being a journalist allowed Munro to see Europe, which influenced his fiction writing later.

He covered the upheavals in the Balkans (1902) and Warsaw (1904), the revolution in St. Petersburg (1905), and eventually moved to Paris in 1907.

Turning to fiction instead, Monroe wrote several short stories for newspapers and collected them in *Not-So-Stories* (1902). Monroe took the pen name Saki, which he used on all his newspapers correspondents and short stories. The name Saki comes from the *Rubaiyat of Omar Khayyam*, a collection of Persian poems from the twelfth century. In the poem, Saki means cupbearer in Farsi, the language of Iran: "And fear not lest Existence closing your / Account, and mine, should know the like no more; / The Eternal Saki from that Bowl has pour'd / Millions of Bubbles like us, and will pour." Like the meaning of his name, Munro, too, would be the cup bearer of stories poured forth for many to enjoy.

With the advent of King Edward VII upon Queen Victoria's death in 1901, a new era, the Edwardian Period, started and was seen by many as a Golden Age of opulence for the rich. However, it was overwrought with lethargy and mediocrity, of which Munro was a scathing critic, often using witty satire. In 1911, he published another collection of short stories *The Chronicles of Clovis*, which also has stories criticized as being anti-Semitic and misogynistic. His first novel, *The Unbearable Bassington*, was written shortly after. 1914 marked the year he published *Beasts and Super-Beasts*, a collection of short stories that contains his most often anthologized and popular story "The Open Window." Like all his previous works, the writing is simple, yet his cynicism and wit are as sharp as ever. The popularity and style of his stories have been compared with those of O. Henry.

He wrote his second novel, *When William Came,* in 1913, a type of alternate history novel which speculated that a British society fell under the invasion of a German emperor named William II. Written before the outbreak of the World War I, the novel is an example of the invasion literature popular at that time, made ever popular by the likes of H.G. Wells, and predicted the German aggression leading to a worldwide conflict.

When the Great War did break out in 1914, Munro enlisted in the army, though he was not required to do so due to his age. On November 14, two years later, he was fighting in the trenches near the northern tip of France, where he was huddling in a shell crater with enemy fire zipping past his head. A sniper's bullet eventually caught him, and he died, another tragic victim of the war.

The Open Window

"My aunt will be down presently, Mr. Nuttel," said a very self-possessed young lady of fifteen; "in the meantime you must try and put up with me."

Framton Nuttel endeavored to say the correct something which should duly flatter the niece of the moment without unduly discounting the aunt that was to come. Privately he doubted more than ever whether these formal visits on a succession of total strangers would do much towards helping the nerve cure which he was supposed to be undergoing.

"I know how it will be," his sister had said when he was preparing to migrate to this rural retreat; "you will bury yourself down there and not speak to a living soul, and your nerves will be worse than ever from moping.[1] I shall just give you letters of introduction to all the people I know there. Some of them, as far as I can remember, were quite nice."

Framton wondered whether Mrs. Sappleton, the lady to whom he was presenting one of the letters of introduction, came into the nice division.

"Do you know many of the people round here?" asked the niece, when she judged that they had had sufficient silent communion.

"Hardly a soul," said Framton. "My sister was staying here, at the rectory,[2] you know, some four years ago, and she gave

---

1. **moping**: sulking; depression
2. **rectory**: a building of a local Christian leader large enough to house his family and other boarders

me letters of introduction to some of the people here."

He made the last statement in a tone of distinct regret.

"Then you know practically nothing about my aunt?" pursued the self-possessed young lady.

"Only her name and address," admitted the caller. He was wondering whether Mrs. Sappleton was in the married or widowed state. An indefinable something about the room seemed to suggest masculine habitation.

"Her great tragedy happened just three years ago," said the child; "that would be since your sister's time."

"Her tragedy?" asked Framton; somehow in this restful country spot tragedies seemed out of place.

"You may wonder why we keep that window wide open on an October afternoon," said the niece, indicating a large French window that opened on to a lawn.

"It is quite warm for the time of the year," said Framton; "but has that window got anything to do with the tragedy?"

"Out through that window, three years ago to a day, her husband and her two young brothers went off for their day's shooting. They never came back. In crossing the moor[3] to their favorite snipe-shooting[4] ground they were all three engulfed in a treacherous piece of bog.[5] It had been that dreadful wet summer, you know, and places that were safe in other years gave way suddenly without warning. Their bodies were never recovered. That was the dreadful part of it." Here the child's voice lost its self-possessed note and became falteringly human. "Poor aunt al-

---

3. **moor**: marsh
4. **snipe**: a small game bird with a long, pointed bill
5. **bog**: grassy area saturated with water so that it becomes spongy and swampy

ways thinks that they will come back some day, they and the little brown spaniel[6] that was lost with them, and walk in at that window just as they used to do. That is why the window is kept open every evening till it is quite dusk. Poor dear aunt, she has often told me how they went out, her husband with his white waterproof coat over his arm, and Ronnie, her youngest brother, singing 'Bertie, why do you bound?' as he always did to tease her, because she said it got on her nerves. Do you know, sometimes on still, quiet evenings like this, I almost get a creepy feeling that they will all walk in through that window – "

She broke off with a little shudder. It was a relief to Framton when the aunt bustled into the room with a whirl of apologies for being late in making her appearance.

"I hope Vera has been amusing you?" she said.

"She has been very interesting," said Framton.

"I hope you don't mind the open window," said Mrs. Sappleton briskly; "my husband and brothers will be home directly from shooting, and they always come in this way. They've been out for snipe in the marshes to-day, so they'll make a fine mess over my poor carpets. So like you men-folk, isn't it?"

She rattled on cheerfully about the shooting and the scarcity of birds, and the prospects for duck in the winter. To Framton it was all purely horrible. He made a desperate but only partially successful effort to turn the talk on to a less ghastly topic; he was conscious that his hostess was giving him only a fragment of her attention, and her eyes were constantly straying past him to the open window and the lawn beyond. It was certainly an unfortunate coincidence that he should have paid his visit on this tragic anniversary.

---

6. **spaniel**: a small bird hunting dog

"The doctors agree in ordering me complete rest, an absence of mental excitement, and avoidance of anything in the nature of violent physical exercise," announced Framton, who labored under the tolerably widespread delusion that total strangers and chance acquaintances are hungry for the least detail of one's ailments and infirmities, their cause and cure. "On the matter of diet they are not so much in agreement," he continued.

"No?" said Mrs. Sappleton, in a voice which only replaced a yawn at the last moment. Then she suddenly brightened into alert attention - but not to what Framton was saying.

"Here they are at last!" she cried. "Just in time for tea, and don't they look as if they were muddy up to the eyes!"

Framton shivered slightly and turned towards the niece with a look intended to convey sympathetic comprehension. The child was staring out through the open window with dazed horror in her eyes. In a chill shock of nameless fear Framton swung round in his seat and looked in the same direction.

In the deepening twilight three figures were walking across the lawn towards the window; they all carried guns under their arms, and one of them was additionally burdened with a white coat hung over his shoulders. A tired brown spaniel kept close at their heels. Noiselessly they neared the house, and then a hoarse young voice chanted out of the dusk: "I said, Bertie, why do you bound?"

Framton grabbed wildly at his stick and hat; the hall-door, the gravel-drive,[7] and the front gate were dimly-noted stages in his headlong retreat. A cyclist coming along the road had to run into the hedge to avoid an imminent collision.

---

7. **gravel-drive**: the gravel driveway (as opposed to a dirt one) that leads from the main road up to a house

"Here we are, my dear," said the bearer of the white mackintosh,[8] coming in through the window; "fairly muddy, but most of it's dry. Who was that who bolted out as we came up?"

"A most extraordinary man, a Mr. Nuttel," said Mrs. Sappleton; "could only talk about his illnesses, and dashed off without a word of good-bye or apology when you arrived. One would think he had seen a ghost."

"I expect it was the spaniel," said the niece calmly; "he told me he had a horror of dogs. He was once hunted into a cemetery somewhere on the banks of the Ganges[9] by a pack of pariah dogs,[10] and had to spend the night in a newly dug grave with the creatures snarling and grinning and foaming just above him. Enough to make anyone their nerve."

Romance at short notice was her speciality.

---

8. **mackintosh**: raincoat
9. **Ganges**: a large river that flows through northern India
10. **pariah dogs**: dogs that have been abandoned and turned wild

Commentary

Saki wrote at the height of the British Empire during the rule of King Edward VII. The upper-class enjoyed several decades of opulence and prosperity. Often when the Edwardian period is mentioned, scenes of garden parties with men in tuxedos escorting women in voluminous dresses and carrying parasols come to mind. The people of England were secure in their position as a world power. They failed to see the threat brewing throughout Europe as other powerful nations vied for economic dominance and national security. Saki, along with other authors such as H.G. Wells, saw England heading for catastrophe, possibly including a worldwide conflict. Enter the short story "The Open Window." The irony becomes evident in this short story when the roots of cruelty creep up into the veneer of a comfortable lifestyle.

To understand exactly why the characters behave the way they do, let's first examine the practices of Edwardian polite society. It was quite common, in fact downright polite, for people who wished to settle into new neighborhoods to visit their neighbors the way Mr. Nuttel does with a so called "letter of recommendation" from mutual acquaintances. This way the neighbors could judge if the newcomer was of "proper company" and fit to live in the neighborhood. Though the practice was common, it carried a sense of xenophobia with it; people were afraid of those who were not like them. They may receive their neighbor politely outwardly, but if any trait was deemed undesirable or did not fit with the status quo, the offending person would eventually have been ostracized. Such a social norm was hard for Saki to accept, being an outsider himself. Born in the far reaches of the Empire, raised by strict aunts, and having a poor health certainly made him feel ill at ease in Victorian and Edwardian society. Such lack of acceptance is revealed wonderfully in this simple tale.

The fifteen-year-old girl puts on the mask of polite society throughout the whole story. She is nothing but congenial, polite, and kind on the surface, yet her treatment of Mr. Nuttel is loathsome. Saki utilizes situational irony that ensnares the reader along with the unwitting Mr. Nuttel, whose name, by the way, is also ironic. He has the appearance and the name to suggest he is a "nut" or crazy, but he is only the unfortunate victim of a girl's one-sided game. The reader, along with Mr. Nuttel, is lead to believe that Mrs. Sappleton is a grieving widow that cannot accept the deaths of her husband and two brothers, and that Mrs. Sappleton is somewhat unstable in mind. When the three hunters return, the reader starts to feel the horror of apparitions suddenly appearing through the open window just as the unsuspecting girl has told it. Horror turns to dramatic irony as the reader realizes that the whole story told is just fiction, yet poor Mr. Nuttel is driven from the house in a state of fractured nerves amplified so many times worse than he arrived in.

The true evil of this genteel girl is found in her intent. The reader may chuckle at such an innocent little joked played on a newcomer, but what she does next clearly reveals her contemptible heart. When asked as to why Mr. Nuttel ran off, the girl, who herself remains nameless and a stranger to the reader, reveals that he has suffered a nervous breakdown. Such a fib will undoubtedly cause not only the Sappletons but also all their acquaintances to keep a large breadth of Mr. Nuttel in the future.

His social life is ended even before it begins.

This fear of foreigners, fear of the unknown, is what drove the invasion literature at the end of the Victorian period and on into the Edwardian. Novels like 1871's *The Battle of Dorking,* which was the first to depict Germany invading England; *Dracula,* a foreign beast of a man "invading" the quiet homes of respectable London ladies; and *War of the Worlds,* creatures from another planet invading England, drove the British alarmism over Empirical expansion. Even Saki's *When William Came* tapped into the national zeitgeist. What Saki seems to do with this story and in others, is show the dark side of such fear and how it can turn innocents into monsters. Indeed, in an anthology entitled *Beasts and Super-Beasts,* "The Open Window" may seem incongruent in a collection of stories about dangerous animals, yet the young girl herself features rather beastly behavior. It would seem that Saki feared with many the imminent outbreak of war, but he also seemed to think that shunning of all outsiders was just as erroneous as sitting complacently as the world plunged into chaos.

Introduction of the Author

James Joyce (1882-1941)

Hailed as one of, if not the greatest writers of the 20th century, James Joyce was born in Dublin, Ireland on February 2, 1882, the oldest of ten children. He was raised by a father, who was known to waste money, and a devout Catholic mother. By the age of six, he was sent to Belvedere College for a Catholic education under Jesuit priests with the hopes that he would later become a priest. Living in Ireland that sought constant liberation from British rule, Joyce eventually left out of the need to distance himself from what he thought of as a losing battle. Though he lived in poverty as an English teacher in several countries, he wrote everyday and, perhaps out of homesickness, often returned to the city of his birth in his works of fiction with such delicacy that a reader who has never visited Dublin would intimately know of all its details. He collected his short stories in his first publication, *Dubliners* (1914), which includes "A Painful Case."

James Joyce is considered the father of stream of consciousness, with Virginia Woolf the mother, a literary form where the author strays as far away from the rules of normal writing to the point where the reader is given the sense that he or she is "reading" the mind of the narrator. Punctuation, quotation marks, and other conventional forms of grammar may be removed to add to the effect. Since the mind wanders as it thinks freely, so does the text of the narrator, often creating confusion. *Dubliners* started to exhibit early forms of stream of consciousness, but not until his semi-autobiographical novel, *A Portrait of the Artist as a Young Man* (1914), and his literary masterpiece, *Ulysses,* (1922) did it come to the fore. *Ulysses* also started out as a short story to be featured in *Dubliners,* but the idea of expanding the story to include the daily life of a man as an anti-heroic journey in imitation of Homer's *Odyssey* turned into a 750+ page book.

Ulysses covered a day in the life, while his next great work of fiction covered the dream ridden haunts of the night in *Finnegan's Wake* (1939). It took over 17 years to write, and Joyce hailed it as the greatest achievement of his profession, having discarded all plot devices and employing stream of consciousness to the maximum. During the writing of this book, Joyce started to go blind, having close friends write what he dictated, much the way the blind Milton would dictate *Paradise Lost.* Joyce also suffered from stomach cramps before he could publish his opus. When it was published, the literary world did not know what to make of it. Only with the study and understanding of stream of consciousness did the genius of the work come out.

As World War II swept through Europe, Joyce feared that all he had worked for would be lost as France, where he was living at the time, became occupied by the Nazi's. He was forced to move to Zurich, Switzerland, where his stomach pains continued. On January 13, 1941, after an operation to remove his ulcer, he quietly passed away after saying his goodbyes to his loved ones. He was 51. Joyce may have died in his writing prime, but the legacy he left behind changed the way we would read and write fiction for ever more.

A Painful Case

Mr. James Duffy lived in Chapelizod[1] because he wished to live as far as possible from the city of which he was a citizen and because he found all the other suburbs of Dublin mean, modern and pretentious. He lived in an old sombre house and from his windows he could look into the disused distillery or upwards along the shallow river[2] on which Dublin is built. The lofty walls of his uncarpeted room were free from pictures. He had himself bought every article of furniture in the room: a black iron bedstead, an iron washstand, four cane chairs, a clothes-rack, a coal-scuttle, a fender[3] and irons and a square table on which lay a double desk. A bookcase had been made in an alcove by means of shelves of white wood. The bed was clothed with white bedclothes and a black and scarlet rug covered the foot. A little hand-mirror hung above the washstand and during the day a white-shaded lamp stood as the sole ornament of the mantelpiece. The books on the white wooden shelves were arranged from below upwards according to bulk. A complete Wordsworth[4] stood at one end of the lowest shelf and a copy of the *Maynooth Catechism*,[5] sewn into the cloth cover of a notebook, stood at one end of the top shelf. Writing materials were

---

1. **Chapelizod**: village three miles west of the center of Dublin
2. **shallow river**: the River Liffey that flows through Dublin and drains into the Dublin bay
3. **fender**: a metal frame placed at the bottom of a fireplace to keep coals from rolling out
4. **a complete Wordsworth**: a collection of William Wordsworth's (1770-1850) poems
5. ***Maynooth Catechism***: an Irish Roman Catholic text for religious instruction

always on the desk. In the desk lay a manuscript translation of Hauptmann's *Michael Kramer*,[6] the stage directions of which were written in purple ink, and a little sheaf of papers held together by a brass pin. In these sheets a sentence was inscribed from time to time and, in an ironical moment, the headline of an advertisement for *Bile Beans*[7] had been pasted on to the first sheet. On lifting the lid of the desk a faint fragrance escaped—the fragrance of new cedar-wood pencils or of a bottle of gum or of an overripe apple which might have been left there and forgotten.

Mr. Duffy abhorred[8] anything which betokened[9] physical or mental disorder. A medieval doctor would have called him saturnine.[10] His face, which carried the entire tale of his years, was of the brown tint of Dublin streets. On his long and rather large head grew dry black hair and a tawny moustache did not quite cover an unamiable mouth. His cheekbones also gave his face a harsh character; but there was no harshness in the eyes which, looking at the world from under their tawny eyebrows, gave the impression of a man ever alert to greet a redeeming instinct in others but often disappointed. He lived at a little distance from his body, regarding his own acts with doubtful side-glasses. He had an odd autobiographical habit which led him to compose in his mind from time to time a short sentence

---

6. *Michael Kramer*: a four act play (1900) written by German poet, novelist, and dramatist Gerhart Hauptmann (1862-1946) detailing the contention between a father and son
7. *Bile* **Beans**: a patented "cure-all" medicine.
8. **abhorred**: hated
9. **betokened**: indicated
10. **saturnine**: gloomy, or dull (a person born under the medieval astrological sign of Saturn)

about himself containing a subject in the third person and a predicate in the past tense. He never gave alms to beggars and walked firmly, carrying a stout hazel.[11]

He had been for many years cashier of a private bank in Baggot Street. Every morning he came in from Chapelizod by tram. At midday he went to Dan Burke's[12] and took his lunch—a bottle of lager beer and a small trayful of arrowroot biscuits. At four o'clock he was set free. He dined in an eating-house in George's Street where he felt himself safe from the society of Dublin's gilded youth[13] and where there was a certain plain honesty in the bill of fare. His evenings were spent either before his landlady's piano or roaming about the outskirts of the city. His liking for Mozart's music brought him sometimes to an opera or a concert: these were the only dissipations of his life.

He had neither companions nor friends, church nor creed. He lived his spiritual life without any communion with others, visiting his relatives at Christmas and escorting them to the cemetery when they died. He performed these two social duties for old dignity's sake but conceded nothing further to the conventions which regulate the civic life. He allowed himself to think that in certain circumstances he would rob his hank[14] but, as these circumstances never arose, his life rolled out evenly—an adventureless tale.

One evening he found himself sitting beside two ladies in the Rotunda.[15] The house, thinly peopled and silent, gave dis-

---

11. **hazel**: a tree of poets in Irish mythology from whence poets plucked wisdom from the nuts and beauty from flowers
12. **Dan Burke**: a pub
13. **gilded youth**: gangs
14. **hank**: an evil habit
15. **Rotunda**: a theater district

tressing prophecy of failure. The lady who sat next him looked round at the deserted house once or twice and then said:

"What a pity there is such a poor house tonight! It's so hard on people to have to sing to empty benches."

He took the remark as an invitation to talk. He was surprised that she seemed so little awkward. While they talked he tried to fix her permanently in his memory. When he learned that the young girl beside her was her daughter he judged her to be a year or so younger than himself. Her face, which must have been handsome, had remained intelligent. It was an oval face with strongly marked features. The eyes were very dark blue and steady. Their gaze began with a defiant note but was confused by what seemed a deliberate swoon of the pupil into the iris, revealing for an instant a temperament of great sensibility. The pupil reasserted itself quickly, this half- disclosed nature fell again under the reign of prudence, and her astrakhan[16] jacket, moulding a bosom of a certain fullness, struck the note of defiance more definitely.

He met her again a few weeks afterwards at a concert in Earlsfort Terrace and seized the moments when her daughter's attention was diverted to become intimate. She alluded once or twice to her husband but her tone was not such as to make the allusion a warning. Her name was Mrs. Sinico. Her husband's great-great-grandfather had come from Leghorn. Her husband was captain of a mercantile boat plying[17] between Dublin and Holland; and they had one child.

Meeting her a third time by accident he found courage to

---

16. **astrakhan**: a central Asian region that produced cloth from the dark fleece of young lambs
17. **ply**: a nautical term meaning to travel (by boat) regularly between two places

make an appointment. She came. This was the first of many meetings; they met always in the evening and chose the most quiet quarters for their walks together. Mr. Duffy, however, had a distaste for underhand ways and, finding that they were compelled to meet stealthily, he forced her to ask him to her house. Captain Sinico encouraged his visits, thinking that his daughter's hand[18] was in question. He had dismissed his wife so sincerely from his gallery of pleasures that he did not suspect that anyone else would take an interest in her. As the husband was often away and the daughter out giving music lessons Mr. Duffy had many opportunities of enjoying the lady's society. Neither he nor she had had any such adventure before and neither was conscious of any incongruity.[19] Little by little he entangled his thoughts with hers. He lent her books, provided her with ideas, shared his intellectual life with her. She listened to all.

Sometimes in return for his theories she gave out some fact of her own life. With almost maternal solicitude[20] she urged him to let his nature open to the full: she became his confessor. He told her that for some time he had assisted at the meetings of an Irish Socialist Party where he had felt himself a unique figure amidst a score of sober workmen in a garret[21] lit by an inefficient oil-lamp. When the party had divided into three sections, each under its own leader and in its own garret, he had discontinued his attendances. The workmen's discussions, he said, were too timorous; the interest they took in the question of wages was inordinate. He felt that they were hard-featured realists and that

---

18. **daughter's hand**: marriage with his daughter
19. **incongruity**: inappropriateness
20. **solicitude**: concern
21. **garret**: a small, shabby attic

they resented an exactitude which was the produce of a leisure not within their reach. No social revolution, he told her, would be likely to strike Dublin for some centuries.

She asked him why did he not write out his thoughts. For what, he asked her, with careful scorn. To compete with phrasemongers,[22] incapable of thinking consecutively for sixty seconds? To submit himself to the criticisms of an obtuse middle class which entrusted its morality to policemen and its fine arts to impresarios?[23]

He went often to her little cottage outside Dublin; often they spent their evenings alone. Little by little, as their thoughts entangled, they spoke of subjects less remote. Her companionship was like a warm soil about an exotic. Many times she allowed the dark to fall upon them, refraining from lighting the lamp. The dark discreet room, their isolation, the music that still vibrated in their ears united them. This union exalted him, wore away the rough edges of his character, emotionalised his mental life. Sometimes he caught himself listening to the sound of his own voice. He thought that in her eyes he would ascend to an angelical stature; and, as he attached the fervent nature of his companion more and more closely to him, he heard the strange impersonal voice which he recognised as his own, insisting on the soul's incurable loneliness. We cannot give ourselves, it said: we are our own. The end of these discourses was that one night during which she had shown every sign of unusual excitement, Mrs. Sinico caught up his hand passionately and pressed it to her cheek.

Mr. Duffy was very much surprised. Her interpretation of his words disillusioned him. He did not visit her for a week, then

---

22. **phrasemongers**: people who use elevated speech to impress others
23. **impresarios**: public entertainment managers

he wrote to her asking her to meet him. As he did not wish their last interview to be troubled by the influence of their ruined confessional they meet in a little cake-shop near the Parkgate. It was cold autumn weather but in spite of the cold they wandered up and down the roads of the Park for nearly three hours. They agreed to break off their intercourse: every bond, he said, is a bond to sorrow. When they came out of the Park they walked in silence towards the tram; but here she began to tremble so violently that, fearing another collapse on her part, he bade her good-bye quickly and left her. A few days later he received a parcel containing his books and music.

Four years passed. Mr. Duffy returned to his even way of life. His room still bore witness of the orderliness of his mind. Some new pieces of music encumbered[24] the music-stand in the lower room and on his shelves stood two volumes by Nietzsche:

Thus Spake Zarathustra and *The Gay Science*.[25] He wrote seldom in the sheaf of papers which lay in his desk. One of his sentences, written two months after his last interview with Mrs. Sinico, read: Love between man and man is impossible because there must not be sexual intercourse and friendship between man and woman is impossible because there must be sexual intercourse.[26] He kept away from concerts lest he should meet her. His father died; the junior partner of the bank retired. And still every morn-

24. **encumbered**: filled to the point of obstructing
25. ***Thus Spake Zarathustra* and *The Gay Science***: philosophical works written by Friedrich Nietzsche (1844-1900), a German philosopher who wrote that "God is dead" and that in the four classes of man there was a "superman" who was a god unto himself. These "supermen" should become like hermits to cure the disease of materialism.
26. **Love between man ... sexual intercourse**: The sentences seem to be Mr. Duffy's interpretation of Nietzsche

ing he went into the city by tram and every evening walked home from the city after having dined moderately in George's Street and read the evening paper for dessert.

One evening as he was about to put a morsel of corned beef and cabbage into his mouth his hand stopped. His eyes fixed themselves on a paragraph in the evening paper which he had propped against the water-carafe. He replaced the morsel of food on his plate and read the paragraph attentively. Then he drank a glass of water, pushed his plate to one side, doubled the paper down before him between his elbows and read the paragraph over and over again. The cabbage began to deposit a cold white grease on his plate. The girl came over to him to ask was his dinner not properly cooked. He said it was very good and ate a few mouthfuls of it with difficulty. Then he paid his bill and went out.

He walked along quickly through the November twilight, his stout hazel stick striking the ground regularly, the fringe of the buff Mail[27] peeping out of a side-pocket of his tight reefer[28] overcoat. On the lonely road which leads from the Parkgate to Chapelizod[29] he slackened his pace. His stick struck the ground less emphatically and his breath, issuing irregularly, almost with a sighing sound, condensed in the wintry air. When he reached his house he went up at once to his bedroom and, taking the paper from his pocket, read the paragraph again by the failing light of the window. He read it not aloud, but moving his lips as a priest does when he reads the prayers Secreto.[30] This

---

27. **buff Mail**: *The Dublin Evening Mail*, a pro-English newspaper printed on light brown paper
28. **tight reefer**: a thick short coat, usually made of wool
29. **from the Parkgate to Chapelizod**: about five and a half kilometer walk
30. **Secreto**: Latin for "set apart"; prayers usually spoken in a low voice

was the paragraph:

DEATH OF A LADY AT SYDNEY PARADE

a painful case

Today at the City of Dublin Hospital the Deputy Coroner (in the absence of Mr. Leverett) held an inquest[31] on the body of Mrs. Emily Sinico, aged forty-three years, who was killed at Sydney Parade Station yesterday evening. The evidence showed that the deceased lady, while attempting to cross the line, was knocked down by the engine of the ten o'clock slow train from Kingstown, thereby sustaining injuries of the head and right side which led to her death. James Lennon, driver of the engine, stated that he had been in the employment of the railway company for fifteen years. On hearing the guard's whistle he set the train in motion and a second or two afterwards brought it to rest in response to loud cries. The train was going slowly.

P. Dunne, railway porter, stated that as the train was about to start he observed a woman attempting to cross the lines. He ran towards her and shouted, but, before he could reach her, she was caught by the buffer of the engine and fell to the ground.

A juror. "You saw the lady fall?"

Witness. "Yes."

Police Sergeant Croly deposed[32] that when he arrived he found the deceased lying on the platform apparently dead. He had the body taken to the waiting-room pending the arrival of the ambulance.

---

31. **inquest**: an inquiry into an unexplained death
32. **deposed**: testified

Constable 57 corroborated.[33]

Dr. Halpin, assistant house surgeon of the City of Dublin Hospital, stated that the deceased had two lower ribs fractured and had sustained severe contusions[34] of the right shoulder. The right side of the head had been injured in the fall. The injuries were not sufficient to have caused death in a normal person. Death, in his opinion, had been probably due to shock and sudden failure of the heart's action.

Mr. H. B. Patterson Finlay, on behalf of the railway company, expressed his deep regret at the accident. The company had always taken every precaution to prevent people crossing the lines except by the bridges, both by placing notices in every station and by the use of patent spring gates at level crossings. The deceased had been in the habit of crossing the lines late at night from platform to platform and, in view of certain other circumstances of the case, he did not think the railway officials were to blame.

Captain Sinico, of Leoville, Sydney Parade, husband of the deceased, also gave evidence. He stated that the deceased was his wife. He was not in Dublin at the time of the accident as he had arrived only that morning from Rotterdam. They had been married for twenty-two years and had lived happily until about two years ago when his wife began to be rather intemperate[35] in her habits.

Miss Mary Sinico said that of late her mother had been in the habit of going out at night to buy spirits.[36] She, witness, had often tried to reason with her mother and had in-

33. **corroborated**: Confirmed
34. **contusions**: injuries without breaking the skin; injuries that occurs under the skin
35. **intemperate**: strange; perhaps she started to over drink
36. **spirits**: an alcoholic drink

> duced her to join a League.[37] She was not at home until an hour after the accident. The jury returned a verdict in accordance with the medical evidence and exonerated[38] Lennon from all blame.
>
> The Deputy Coroner said it was a most painful case, and expressed great sympathy with Captain Sinico and his daughter. He urged on the railway company to take strong measures to prevent the possibility of similar accidents in the future. No blame attached to anyone.

Mr. Duffy raised his eyes from the paper and gazed out of his window on the cheerless evening landscape. The river lay quiet beside the empty distillery and from time to time a light appeared in some house on the Lucan road. What an end! The whole narrative of her death revolted him and it revolted him to think that he had ever spoken to her of what he held sacred. The threadbare phrases, the inane expressions of sympathy, the cautious words of a reporter won over to conceal the details of a commonplace vulgar death attacked his stomach. Not merely had she degraded herself; she had degraded him. He saw the squalid tract of her vice, miserable and malodorous.[39] His soul's companion! He thought of the hobbling wretches whom he had seen carrying cans and bottles to be filled by the barman. Just God, what an end! Evidently she had been unfit to live, without any strength of purpose, an easy prey to habits, one of the wrecks on which civilisation has been reared. But that she could have sunk so low! Was it possible he had deceived himself so utterly

37. **League**: an association like Alcohols Anonymous where those who enter promise to never drink again
38. **exonerated**: relieved
39. **malodorous**: foul

about her? He remembered her outburst of that night and interpreted it in a harsher sense than he had ever done. He had no difficulty now in approving of the course he had taken.

As the light failed and his memory began to wander he thought her hand touched his. The shock which had first attacked his stomach was now attacking his nerves. He put on his overcoat and hat quickly and went out. The cold air met him on the threshold; it crept into the sleeves of his coat. When he came to the public-house[40] at Chapelizod Bridge he went in and ordered a hot punch.

The proprietor served him obsequiously[41] but did not venture to talk. There were five or six workingmen in the shop discussing the value of a gentleman's estate in County Kildare. They drank at intervals from their huge pint tumblers and smoked, spitting often on the floor and sometimes dragging the sawdust over their spits with their heavy boots. Mr. Duffy sat on his stool and gazed at them, without seeing or hearing them. After a while they went out and he called for another punch. He sat a long time over it. The shop was very quiet. The proprietor sprawled on the counter reading the Herald and yawning. Now and again a tram was heard swishing along the lonely road outside.

As he sat there, living over his life with her and evoking alternately the two images in which he now conceived her, he realised that she was dead, that she had ceased to exist, that she had become a memory. He began to feel ill at ease. He asked himself what else could he have done. He could not have carried on a comedy of deception with her; he could not have lived with her openly. He had done what seemed to him best. How was

---

40. **public-house**: an inn
41. **obsequiously**: dutifully

he to blame? Now that she was gone he understood how lonely her life must have been, sitting night after night alone in that room. His life would be lonely too until he, too, died, ceased to exist, became a memory—if anyone remembered him.

It was after nine o'clock when he left the shop. The night was cold and gloomy. He entered the Park by the first gate and walked along under the gaunt[42] trees. He walked through the bleak alleys where they had walked four years before. She seemed to be near him in the darkness. At moments he seemed to feel her voice touch his ear, her hand touch his. He stood still to listen. Why had he withheld life from her? Why had he sentenced her to death? He felt his moral nature falling to pieces.

When he gained the crest of the Magazine Hill he halted and looked along the river towards Dublin, the lights of which burned redly[43] and hospitably in the cold night. He looked down the slope and, at the base, in the shadow of the wall of the Park, he saw some human figures lying. Those venal[44] and furtive loves[45] filled him with despair. He gnawed the rectitude[46] of his life; he felt that he had been outcast from life's feast. One human being had seemed to love him and he had denied her life and happiness: he had sentenced her to ignominy,[47] a death of shame. He knew that the prostrate creatures down by the wall were watching him and wished him gone. No one wanted him; he was outcast from life's feast. He turned his eyes to the grey

---

42. **gaunt**: thin
43. **the lights of which burned redly**: refers to the red-light district- a common place of prostitution
44. **venal**: to get at a price
45. **furtive**: secretive; Mr. Duffy is witnessing prostitution
46. **rectitude**: morality
47. **ignominy**: dishonor

gleaming river, winding along towards Dublin. Beyond the river he saw a goods train winding out of Kingsbridge Station, like a worm with a fiery head winding through the darkness, obstinately[48] and laboriously. It passed slowly out of sight; but still he heard in his ears the laborious drone of the engine reiterating the syllables of her name.

He turned back the way he had come, the rhythm of the engine pounding in his ears. He began to doubt the reality of what memory told him. He halted under a tree and allowed the rhythm to die away. He could not feel her near him in the darkness nor her voice touch his ear. He waited for some minutes listening. He could hear nothing: the night was perfectly silent. He listened again: perfectly silent. He felt that he was alone.

---

48. **obstinately**: stubbornly

Commentary

James Joyce's short story "A Painful Case" starts off introducing the protagonist, Mr. James Duffy, as a lonely, overly organized man who has failed to recognize his own misanthropy until it is too late. The limited third person point of view allows us, the reader, to slowly discover this revelation with Mr. Duffy, but we are given a clue early with the first sentence. We are told that he has sequestered himself far from the city, and other suburbs, which he finds "modern and pretentious." He may not have realized it yet, but he is agonizingly alone. The limited point of view also allows us access to Mr. Duffy's thoughts and feelings with the ability to see further into the future than the protagonist. In other words, we can see where he makes his mistakes before he does, and we can even see his pathetic lifestyle long before he himself realizes it. Furthermore, we can even shake our heads when he fails to do anything about his lonely predicament and returns to the same state he was at in the beginning—alone.

We are introduced to Mr. Duffy's dreary abode early in the story. His room is not only dull, but it has a rather dismal view of a distillery and the river that runs through Dublin. Highlighting such depression is the fact that his walls are bare of any pictures, especially those of family or loved ones. James Joyce uses the colors of yellow and brown, as he does throughout other stories in *The Dubliners*, to emphasize the decay that occurs with the characters and, in "A Painful Case," the decay that has set into Mr. Duffy's life and surroundings.

Mr. Duffy hates any form of "physical or mental disorder." He is stuck in stagnation, and for any person this is death; this is the decay, as indicated by his face having a "brown tint of Dublin streets." Humankind should always strive to move forward, but Mr. Duffy has managed to stall his life into comfortable inaction. He feels secure in a rut of daily apathy—until he meets Mrs. Sinico. Though he had met her several times by chance, when she starts to take interest in him, he insists upon meeting at her house. With the blessing of Captain Sinico, Mr. Duffy unexpectedly starts to open up to her, telling her all. He fails to realize that his orderly world is coming unraveled, and that Mrs. Sinico is drawing him into the world of humanity and emotions. He begins to be happy. We, the reader, can see that he makes a huge mistake by listening to his stuffy impersonal inner voice that says, "We cannot give ourselves, it said: we are our own." Thus, he rebuffs her most wanting advances when she presses his hand to her cheek, and he turns inward again to old familiarity of his ordered, dreary, terribly lonely life. He even fails to rekindle his humanity when he quickly calls off their association and leaves her before she faints, so he won't have to deal with her any more on an emotional level.

Here, I feel, Joyce is commenting on the failings of modern existence. Mr. Duffy returns to his routines, and has started to read philosophy, especially that of Nietzsche. According to Nietzsche in *Thus Spake Zarathustra*, individuals in society must strive to become *Übermensch* or a "Supermen" in the wake of the death of God. If there is no God, then there is no morality; thus, a Superman must fill the void. A Nietzschean Superman is a person who has overcome himself, his own humanity. Just as the evolutionary chain led from ape to humanity, the next step is from humanity to Superman. Just as we laugh and scoff at the notion of coming from apes, so too will a Superman laugh at the idea of coming from man. Spiritual humanity longs for the heavenly, often otherworldly, hereafter, while the grounded Superman remains fixed firmly to the earth, living a life of certainty, for he has put behind him all weak possibilities. To others, such a person may appear inhuman because he is not ruled by anything "holy" or "good." Sound familiar? I read Mr. Duffy as a Nietzschean *Übermensch* who suffers because he lives beyond any "normal" way of living; he suffers because he does not feel at home in the world, and never will until the world catches up with him and his own morality.

Then comes the "painful case." Mr. Duffy reads in a brown newspaper that Mrs. Sinico is dead. The reader is given her point of view through the clever crafting of the newspaper, so Joyce does not have to break his limited third person narrative. The cause of her death is not known, but the reader, along with Mr. Duffy, knows that the sudden ending of their Platonic affair has led to her depression and suicide. Since Captain Sinico had "dismissed his wife so sincerely from his gallery of pleasures that he did not suspect that anyone else would take an interest in her," she was alone once again in the world.

Mr. Duffy's initial reaction is that of a Nietzschean Superman—disgust at such depravity and weakness. A Superman is someone who can overcome any obstacle; Mrs. Sinico chose to allow her obstacle to overcome her. To Nietzsche, and to some extent Mr. Duffy, this is a sign of an impoverished life; a life that rejects the immediate world by setting all hopes and dreams on another better world. Thus, she commits suicide. Then Mr. Duffy starts to realize that he is actually suffering from the same symptoms as Mrs. Sinico—loneliness and regret. He finds himself having an epiphany, as is common with most protagonists in *The*

Dubliners. "He felt his moral nature falling to pieces," which is something that should not happen to a Nietzschean *Übermensch.* He sees himself as an outcast from humanity; he sees himself as inhuman. And for the first time in his life, he feels alone. In his attempt to be a Superman, he failed to overcome the one obstacle to make him superior—being human.

Introduction of the Author

Virginia Woolf *(1882-1941)*

As one of the founders of the modernist movement and one of the most influential female authors of the twentieth century, Adeline Virginia Stephen was born in London to a family well immersed in the Arts. Her father, Sir Leslie Stephen, was a well respected author and literary critic, and her mother was a model for Pre-Raphaelite painters. Educated at home by her parents and given full access to her father's library, Virginia later lamented never being educated formally and losing out on all the fun physical activities busy children do. Both her father and mother were widowed and remarried. Her father had a daughter from his previous marriage, Laura, and her mother had three children from hers: Herbert, George, and Stella. Virginia's family life was full of tragedy that took her to the edge of sanity; she would later recount how Gerald sexually abused her; her mother died when she was just a teenager with Stella taking matrimonial duties only to die two years later; Leslie died slowly of a stomach cancer; and when her brother by blood died at the age of six, she succumbed to a psychological break.

Virginia eventually joined an elite group of writers called the Bloomsbury Group in 1899. It was established when middle class writers from Cambridge, England, including Leonard Sidney Woolf, were introduced to Virginia and her sister in Bloomsbury, central London. They met together often to discuss writing, philosophy, and art to name a few. Through their close knit society they extended their view of modernism. Many within the group married each other, Virginia and Leonard included, and most writers with the exception of E.M. Forster found literary success rather late. Not until World War I in 1914 did the Bloomsbury view of modernism come to an end.

When Virginia was 22 years old, her father passed away, and she moved into a house with her surviving sister and two brothers. A year later she started to write professionally and submitted articles to the *Times Literary Supplement*, a weekly literary review paper, her first article being about the Brontë sisters' literary residence, Haworth. Her love for literature continued throughout her life. As a type of pilgrimage, she visited Greece in 1906 with a copy of Homer's *Odyssey* in hand. Her next great adventure was to marry at the age of 30 Leonard Woolf, who had become an established author in his own right.

In 1912, Virginia and Leonard established as a hobby Hogarth Press, their own publishing press by which they first printed titles by hand. Many of their titles included not only those of their Bloomsbury group but also T.S. Eliot's *The Wasteland* (1924), Sigmund Freud's works, and translations of foreign books. Virginia and Leonard, as were all of the Bloomsbury Group, were against World War II; Leonard was not called to fight due to a trembling in his hands, but both had agreed to kill themselves if the Nazi's ever annexed London and they were captured.

Though Virginia Woolf wrote feminist writings, essays (over 500), and many short stories, she is especially remembered for her novels. Her first novel, *The Voyage Out*, was published in 1915, followed by *Jacob's Room* (1922) and *Mrs. Dalloway* (1925). Her following two novels, *To the Lighthouse* (1927), and *The Waves* (1931), established her as one of the foremost writers of modernism, which experimented with exploring the highly private inner self and often employed the stream of consciousness technique. It is probably her best known novel, *Orlando* (1928), that she receives the most recognition. Ultimately, Virginia had wanted it to be the start of a new trend of combining biography with fiction, though it never caught on. It is seen as the epitome of women's literature dealing with women's issues and even the taboo concept of lesbians without causing any scandal. Virginia originally wrote it as a way to show her love and affection for a woman she had a lesbian affair with, the novelist/poet Vita Sackville-West, who appeared on the covers of the first editions dressed as the male Orlando.

With the advent of World War II in 1939, Virginia slipped in and out of depression. Though there was no diagnosis at the time, modern doctors have classified her sickness as bipolar disorder, which accompanies mood swings and depression. The Nazi bombing of London that lasted 57 nights and resulted in total devastation of the city, and harsh criticism surrounding her then recently published non-fiction works pushed her further into depression with no way out. On March 28, 1941, less than a month before the bombing of London ceased, Virginia Woolf filled her pockets with stones and, walking into the river near her house, committed suicide. Her body was not found until 28 days later. Her suicide note left for her husband has been analyzed and to this day has influenced how critics view her works: "I feel certain that I am going mad again. I feel we can't go through another of those terrible times. And I shan't recover this time. I begin to hear voices, and I can't concentrate. So I am doing what seems the best thing to do.[1]"

---

1. From Virginia Woolf's suicide note

The Mark on the Wall

Perhaps it was the middle of January in the present year that I first looked up and saw the mark on the wall. In order to fix a date it is necessary to remember what one saw. So now I think of the fire; the steady film of yellow light upon the page of my book; the three chrysanthemums in the round glass bowl on the mantelpiece.[1] Yes, it must have been the winter time, and we had just finished our tea, for I remember that I was smoking a cigarette when I looked up and saw the mark on the wall for the first time. I looked up through the smoke of my cigarette and my eye lodged for a moment upon the burning coals, and that old fancy of the crimson flag flapping from the castle tower came into my mind, and I thought of the cavalcade of red knights riding up the side of the black rock. Rather to my relief the sight of the mark interrupted the fancy, for it is an old fancy, an automatic fancy, made as a child perhaps. The mark was a small round mark, black upon the white wall, about six or seven inches above the mantelpiece.

How readily our thoughts swarm upon a new object, lifting it a little way, as ants carry a blade of straw so feverishly, and then leave it.... If that mark was made by a nail, it can't have been for a picture, it must have been for a miniature the miniature of a lady with white powdered curls, powder-dusted cheeks, and lips like red carnations. A fraud of course, for the people who had this house before us would have chosen pictures in

---

1. **mantelpiece**: the ledge that frames a fireplace and upon which one places knickknacks

that way an old picture for an old room. That is the sort of people they were very interesting people, and I think of them so often, in such queer places, because one will never see them again, never know what happened next. They wanted to leave this house because they wanted to change their style of furniture, so he said, and he was in process of saying that in his opinion art should have ideas behind it when we were torn asunder, as one is torn from the old lady about to pour out tea and the young man about to hit the tennis ball in the back garden of the suburban villa as one rushes past in the train.

But as for that mark, I'm not sure about it; I don't believe it was made by a nail after all; it's too big, too round, for that. I might get up, but if I got up and looked at it, ten to one I shouldn't be able to say for certain; because once a thing's done, no one ever knows how it happened. Oh! dear me, the mystery of life; The inaccuracy of thought! The ignorance of humanity! To show how very little control of our possessions we have what an accidental affair this living is after all our civilization let me just count over a few of the things lost in one lifetime, beginning, for that seems always the most mysterious of losses what cat would gnaw, what rat would nibble three pale blue canisters of book-binding tools? Then there were the bird cages, the iron hoops,[2] the steel skates, the Queen Anne coal-scuttle,[3] the bagatelle[4] board, the hand organ all gone, and jewels, too. Opals

---

2. **iron hoop**: a toy hoop that children roll across the ground and guide with a stick
3. **Queen Anne coal-scuttle**: a small container that held coal for an indoor coal burning heater; named after the Queen Anne style that utilized only strait edges and square frames with no curves
4. **bagatelle**: a type of board game similar to billiards but smaller and with a rounded end

and emeralds, they lie about the roots of turnips. What a scraping paring affair it is to be sure! The wonder is that I've any clothes on my back, that I sit surrounded by solid furniture at this moment. Why, if one wants to compare life to anything, one must liken it to being blown through the Tube[5] at fifty miles an hour landing at the other end without a single hairpin in one's hair! Shot out at the feet of God entirely naked! Tumbling head over heels in the asphodel meadows[6] like brown paper parcels pitched down a shoot in the post office! With one's hair flying back like the tail of a race-horse. Yes, that seems to express the rapidity of life, the perpetual waste and repair; all so casual, all so haphazard....

But after life. The slow pulling down of thick green stalks so that the cup of the flower, as it turns over, deluges one with purple and red light. Why, after all, should one not be born there as one is born here, helpless, speechless, unable to focus one's eyesight, groping at the roots of the grass, at the toes of the Giants? As for saying which are trees, and which are men and women, or whether there are such things, that one won't be in a condition to do for fifty years or so. There will be nothing but spaces of light and dark, intersected by thick stalks, and rather higher up perhaps, rose-shaped blots of an indistinct colour dim pinks and blues which will, as time goes on, become more definite, become I don't know what....

And yet that mark on the wall is not a hole at all. It may even be caused by some round black substance, such as a small rose leaf, left over from the summer, and I, not being a very vigilant housekeeper look at the dust on the mantelpiece, for exam-

---

5. **the Tube**: the London underground or subway system

6. **asphodel meadows**: a field of asphodel, yellow flowers

ple, the dust which, so they say, buried Troy[7] three times over, only fragments of pots utterly refusing annihilation, as one can believe.

The tree outside the window taps very gently on the pane.... I want to think quietly, calmly, spaciously, never to be interrupted, never to have to rise from my chair, to slip easily from one thing to another, without any sense of hostility, or obstacle. I want to sink deeper and deeper, away from the surface, with its hard separate facts. To steady myself, let me catch hold of the first idea that passes.... Shakespeare.... Well, he will do as well as another. A man who sat himself solidly in an arm-chair, and looked into the fire, so a shower of ideas fell perpetually from some very high Heaven down through his mind. He leant his forehead on his hand, and people, looking in through the open door, for this scene is supposed to take place on a summer's evening but how dull this is, this historical fiction! It doesn't interest me at all. I wish I could hit upon a pleasant track of thought, a track indirectly reflecting credit upon myself, for those are the pleasantest thoughts, and very frequent even in the minds of modest mouse-coloured people, who believe genuinely that they dislike to hear their own praises. They are not thoughts directly praising oneself; that is the beauty of them; they are thoughts like this:

"And then I came into the room. They were discussing botany. I said how I'd seen a flower growing on a dust heap on the site of an old house in Kingsway. The seed, I said, must have been sown in the reign of Charles the First.[8] What flowers grew

---

7. **Troy**: the Trojan city decimated by the Greeks during the mythological Trojan War as recounted in Homer's *The Iliad*; the ruins of the real Troy now believed to be located in present day Turkey

8. **Charles the First**: (1600-1649) King of England, Scotland, and Ireland 1625-1649

in the reign of Charles the First?" I asked (but I don't remember the answer). Tall flowers with purple tassels to them perhaps. And so it goes on. All the time I'm dressing up the figure of myself in my own mind, lovingly, stealthily, not openly adoring it, for if I did that, I should catch myself out, and stretch my hand at once for a book in self-protection. Indeed, it is curious how instinctively one protects the image of oneself from idolatry or any other handling that could make it ridiculous, or too unlike the original to be believed in any longer. Or is it not so very curious after all? It is a matter of great importance. Suppose the looking glass smashes, the image disappears, and the romantic figure with the green of forest depths all about it is there no longer, but only that shell of a person which is seen by other people what an airless, shallow, bald, prominent world it becomes! A world not to be lived in. As we face each other in omnibuses[9] and underground railways we are looking into the mirror; that accounts for the vagueness, the gleam of glassiness, in our eyes. And the novelists in future will realize more and more the importance of these reflections, for of course there is not one reflection but an almost infinite number; those are the depths they will explore, those the phantoms they will pursue, leaving the description of reality more and more out of their stories, taking a knowledge of it for granted, as the Greeks did and Shakespeare perhaps but these generalizations are very worthless. The military sound of the word is enough. It recalls leading articles, cabinet ministers a whole class of things indeed which as a child one thought the thing itself, the standard thing, the real thing, from which one could not depart save at the risk of nameless damnation. Generalizations bring back somehow Sunday in London, Sunday afternoon walks,

---

9. **omnibus**: a bus; omni = for all, and bus = carriage

Sunday luncheons, and also ways of speaking of the dead, clothes, and habits like the habit of sitting all together in one room until a certain hour, although nobody liked it. There was a rule for everything. The rule for tablecloths at that particular period was that they should be made of tapestry with little yellow compartments marked upon them, such as you may see in photographs of the carpets in the corridors of the royal palaces. Tablecloths of a different kind were not real tablecloths. How shocking, and yet how wonderful it was to discover that these real things, Sunday luncheons, Sunday walks, country houses, and tablecloths were not entirely real, were indeed half phantoms, and the damnation which visited the disbeliever in them was only a sense of illegitimate freedom. What now takes the place of those things I wonder, those real standard things? Men perhaps, should you be a woman; the masculine point of view which governs our lives, which sets the standard, which establishes Whitaker's Table of Precedency,[10] which has become, I suppose, since the war half a phantom to many men and women, which soon, one may hope, will be laughed into the dustbin where the phantoms go, the mahogany sideboards and the Landseer prints,[11] Gods and Devils, Hell and so forth, leaving us all with an intoxicating sense of illegitimate freedom if freedom exists....

In certain lights that mark on the wall seems actually to project from the wall. Nor is it entirely circular. I cannot be sure,

10. **Whitaker's Table of Precedency**: instructions on the finer points of seating guests at social engagements according to social hierarchy; found in Whitaker's Almanack

11. **Landseer prints**: copies of painting created by Edwin Henry Landseer (1802-1873), a famous wildlife painter

but it seems to cast a perceptible shadow, suggesting that if I ran my finger down that strip of the wall it would, at a certain point, mount and descend a small tumulus, a smooth tumulus like those barrows[12] on the South Downs[13] which are, they say, either tombs or camps. Of the two I should prefer them to be tombs, desiring melancholy like most English people, and finding it natural at the end of a walk to think of the bones stretched beneath the turf.... There must be some book about it. Some antiquary[14] must have dug up those bones and given them a name.... What sort of a man is an antiquary, I wonder? Retired Colonels for the most part, I daresay, leading parties of aged labourers to the top here, examining clods of earth and stone, and getting into correspondence with the neighbouring clergy, which, being opened at breakfast time, gives them a feeling of importance, and the comparison of arrow-heads necessitates cross-country journeys to the county towns, an agreeable necessity both to them and to their elderly wives, who wish to make plum jam or to clean out the study, and have every reason for keeping that great question of the camp or the tomb in perpetual suspension, while the Colonel himself feels agreeably philosophic in accumulating evidence on both sides of the question. It is true that he does finally incline to believe in the camp; and, being opposed, indites[15] a pamphlet which he is about to read at the quarterly meeting of the local society when a stroke lays him low, and his last conscious thoughts are not of wife or child, but of the camp and that arrowhead there,

---

12. **barrow**: a tomb that resembles a small hill
13. **South Downs**: a fairly unpopulated area in South England that has Neolithic remains and is popular for trekking
14. **antiquary**: a person who deals and collects antiques
15. **indites**: dictates (now obsolete); composes

which is now in the case at the local museum, together with the foot of a Chinese murderess, a handful of Elizabethan nails, a great many Tudor clay pipes, a piece of Roman pottery, and the wine-glass that Nelson drank out of proving I really don't know what.

No, no, nothing is proved, nothing is known. And if I were to get up at this very moment and ascertain that the mark on the wall is really what shall we say? the head of a gigantic old nail, driven in two hundred years ago, which has now, owing to the patient attrition of many generations of housemaids, revealed its head above the coat of paint, and is taking its first view of modern life in the sight of a white-walled fire-lit room, what should I gain? Knowledge? Matter for further speculation? I can think sitting still as well as standing up. And what is knowledge? What are our learned men save the descendants of witches and hermits who crouched in caves and in woods brewing herbs, interrogating shrew-mice and writing down the language of the stars? And the less we honour them as our superstitions dwindle and our respect for beauty and health of mind increases.... Yes, one could imagine a very pleasant world. A quiet, spacious world, with the flowers so red and blue in the open fields. A world without professors or specialists or house-keepers with the profiles of policemen, a world which one could slice with one's thought as a fish slices the water with his fin, grazing the stems of the water-lilies, hanging suspended over nests of white sea eggs.... How peaceful it is down here, rooted in the centre of the world and gazing up through the grey waters, with their sudden gleams of light, and their reflections if it were not for Whitaker's Almanack[16] if it were not for the Table of Precedency!

---

16. **Whitaker's Almanack**: a all-in-one reference book published yearly; first published by Joseph Whitaker in 1868

I must jump up and see for myself what that mark on the wall really is a nail, a rose-leaf, a crack in the wood?

Here is nature once more at her old game of self- preservation. This train of thought, she perceives, is threatening mere waste of energy, even some collision with reality, for who will ever be able to lift a finger against Whitaker's Table of Precedency? The Archbishop of Canterbury is followed by the Lord High Chancellor; the Lord High Chancellor is followed by the Archbishop of York. Everybody follows somebody, such is the philosophy of Whitaker; and the great thing is to know who follows whom. Whitaker knows, and let that, so Nature counsels, comfort you, instead of enraging you; and if you can't be comforted, if you must shatter this hour of peace, think of the mark on the wall.

I understand Nature's game her prompting to take action as a way of ending any thought that threatens to excite or to pain. Hence, I suppose, comes our slight contempt for men of action men, we assume, who don't think. Still, there's no harm in putting a full stop to one's disagreeable thoughts by looking at a mark on the wall.

Indeed, now that I have fixed my eyes upon it, I feel that I have grasped a plank in the sea; I feel a satisfying sense of reality which at once turns the two Archbishops and the Lord High Chancellor to the shadows of shades. Here is something definite, something real. Thus, waking from a midnight dream of horror, one hastily turns on the light and lies quiescent, worshipping the chest of drawers, worshipping solidity, worshipping reality, worshipping the impersonal world which is a proof of some existence other than ours. That is what one wants to be sure of.... Wood is a pleasant thing to think about. It comes from a tree; and trees grow, and we don't know how they grow. For years and years they grow, without paying any attention to us, in meadows, in forests, and by the side of rivers all things one likes to think about. The cows swish their tails beneath them on hot afternoons; they paint rivers so green that when a moorhen[17] dives one expects to see its feathers all green when it comes up again. I like to think of the fish balanced against the stream like flags blown out; and of water-beetles slowly raising domes of mud upon the bed of the river. I like to think of the tree itself: first the close dry sensation of being wood; then the grinding of the storm; then the slow, delicious ooze of sap. I like to think of it, too, on winter's nights standing in the empty field with all leaves close-furled, nothing tender exposed to the iron bullets of the moon, a naked mast upon an earth that goes tumbling, tumbling, all night long. The song of birds must sound very loud and strange in June; and how cold the feet of insects must feel upon it, as they make laborious progresses up the creases of the bark, or sun themselves upon the thin green awning of the leaves, and look straight in front of them with diamond-cut red eyes.... One by one the fibres snap beneath the immense cold pressure of the earth, then the last storm comes and, falling, the highest branches drive deep into the ground again. Even so, life isn't done with; there are a million patient, watchful lives still for a tree, all over the world, in bedrooms, in ships, on the pavement, lining rooms, where men and women sit after tea, smoking cigarettes. It is full of peaceful thoughts, happy thoughts, this tree. I should like to take each one separately but something is getting in the way.... Where was I? What has it all been about? A tree? A river? The Downs? Whitaker's Almanack? The fields of asphodel? I can't remember a thing. Everything's moving, fall-

17. **moorhen**: a medium sized water bird

ing, slipping, vanishing.... There is a vast upheaval of matter. Someone is standing over me and saying

"I'm going out to buy a newspaper."

"Yes?"

"Though it's no good buying newspapers.... Nothing ever happens. Curse this war;[18] God damn this war!... All the same, I don't see why we should have a snail on our wall."

Ah, the mark on the wall! It was a snail.

---

18. **war**: World War II; referencing the London Blitz, the daily bombardment of London by the Nazi's

Commentary

Virginia Woolf's 3,381 word short story "The Mark on the Wall" can be summarized in only 20 words: a woman sees a mark on the wall and ponders what it is until it's revealed to be a snail. It is not much of a story; in fact, there is not even a plot. What significance does such a story hold? It is a study in the personal thought process of a woman paring away the hours, even days, during the World War II bombing of London. The background action of the war is not even mentioned until the very end and has no effect upon the story. The logical flow of the story is not to reveal plot but to experiment in stream of consciousness, a writing technique that attempts to put into words the logical order of synaptic chaos that occurs in an individual's mind.

Stream of consciousness attempts to bring into awareness the jumbling of thoughts, sensations, memories, associations, and reflections that occur in the personal and private mind. Everyone has experienced the sudden and irrational trains of thought that leads from one seemingly unrelated idea to another. Stream of consciousness is a literary convention to try and create a linear plot that these chaotic thought patterns meander around.

Woolf mentions in the second paragraph "How readily our thoughts swarm upon a new object, lifting it a little way, as ants carry a blade of straw so feverishly, and then leave it." So too does the thought process, scurrying in all directions as ants, yet there is a purpose to the supposed madness of the ants. The narrator glances upon a mark on the wall and contemplates what it could actually be. She first deduces the mark as a nail that once supported a painting. She quickly dismisses the idea as her thought shifts to the previous occupant of the house, his inclinations, taste for furniture, and theory on art. Notice how her mind shifts from the interior of the house, then to the previous owner's opinion in art, to their parting, and finally to images seen out of the window of a speeding train: "he was in process of saying that in his opinion art should have ideas behind it when we were torn asunder, as one is torn from the old lady about to pour out tea and the young man about to hit the tennis ball in the back garden of the suburban villa as one rushes past in the train." The connection of the events seems tenuous at best, but perfectly rational in context of how one point of thought leads to another unrelated thought—their parting was as sudden as smashing a tennis ball; and such an image is remembered in context of a flashing memory.

She returns to the mark on the wall and ponders the inaccuracy of thought and compares it to the loss of fleeting possessions. Thoughts and memories are just as fleeting as the junk collected and forgotten over a lifetime; that one is never certain about anything in the world as the narrator is uncertain about the mark on the wall. Perhaps she will never know what it is, or if it is even worth finding out. This ultimately leads to her contemplation on death and how it should be no different than birth. Upon waking after death, one is just as clueless as a babe and in perpetual education over the next fifty years or so.

A tree scratches at her window and distracts her thoughts into another direction. She wishes to fall into a deeper thought away from the mundaneness of her present thoughts and to latch onto a more practical one; thus, she thinks of Shakespeare. However, his creative inventiveness does not interest her. What does interest her is to tell herself a story, which just as quickly flutters away, for she is not writing but thinking, and such thoughts are fleeting. Since she is a part of the story, her mind latches onto self-identity and self-perception. Since all thoughts are attached to the senses, light on the wall draws her eyes back to the mark again, dragging her thoughts back to the origin of the story.

She contemplates the physical aspects of the mark that draws her consciousness to similar shapes: graves and tombs. Thus, she again investigates the idea of death only to have her thoughts shift to the people who would write about it. She then moves into the realm of the antiquary and scholarship. One such scholar, who wishes to prove that mounds are not graves but camps, is struck by a heart attack and dies before he can present his paper. His life is as fleeting as the narrator's thoughts.

The narrator thus concludes, "Nothing is proved, nothing is known." What is knowledge? If she were to stand and through the empirical method ascertain the nature of the mark, what would she gain? Nothing. Knowledge is what others tell it to be. The mark exists on the wall to inspire the thoughts of the narrator. She creates her own form of knowledge. Professors, books, and wise men always tell her what knowledge is. For example, what is a tree? It is actually not so simple an answer. To her it is many concrete details: the bark, the sap, and leaves; but it is also experiences and memories associated with many different trees. Then trees are cut down and turned into a million other objects like ships and furniture that people sit around and use and have a million more experiences. She is ready to enter the world of ideas and explore it further when her husband stands over her. He curses the war and the snail on the wall. To him it is an annoyance, but to the narrator it has led her through the maze of her thoughts and memories on a journey both strange and exhilarating. Through stream of consciousness, the reader, too, is able to follow the narrator on the same journey and experience her thoughts in completely different ways.

Knowledge is boundless, and experience eternal. There is no boundary to thoughts and imagination. Contemplate a mark on the wall and be surprised at where the journey takes you.

Introduction of the Author

H. G. Wells (1866-1946)

Best known as the father of English science fiction, Herbert George Wells was born into a poor middle class family of six. At the age of eight he broke his leg and was confined to a bed where he started reading profusely to pass the time. At this time his passion for stories was sparked as well as his determination to become a writer. However, his schooling was often erratic and of very common stock. To help support the family, Wells became a draper's apprentice at the age of 15, where he experienced firsthand the unfair distribution of wealth that would become a foundation for his later foray into socialism. Labor was not the calling for Wells; he had failed miserably as a draper and later as a chemist's assistant. He did not fail, however, at reading, which he spent a considerable amount of time doing.

When Wells turned seventeen, he started teaching at a grammar school to support his own further education—he secured a scholarship to graduate with a degree in biology. He began his rise into social reformation in earnest by joining debate teams and giving lectures. He even co-founded the *Science School Journal* were he could express his views and publish his short stories. In fact, the early form of his famous novel *The Time Machine* (1895) appeared in this journal entitled "The Chronic Argonauts." It was the first story to mention a time travel machine. Though Wells studied both biology and physics rather successfully, he failed to secure a scholarship his final year because he did not pass biology, which he had little interest in. Not having the money, Wells could not continue his studies. Not until 1890 did he finally earn a degree in zoology from an external degree program out of the University of London.

Wells will forever be remembered for his writing. His prose was considered highly futurist at the time, and he often predicted events and technology that would eventually come to pass. Writing at the turn of the century, he foresaw societies using trains and cars that would result in cities emptying into mass suburbs; the ultimate defeat of German aggression; an establishment of a European Union; and world wars with aerial bombings and the use of chemicals in warfare. He, however, could not foresee any practical use for the submarine and airplanes not being feasibly created until after 1950. He went on to publish 100 books in almost every genre, with half of them novels; some of them were to become the most respected of science fiction novels: *The Time Machine*, *The Island of Doctor Moreau* (1896), *The Invisible Man* (1897), *The War of the Worlds* (1898).

The Time Machine was his first novel where he parodied the English class structure that he grew to hate as a teenager and abhorred the rest of his life. In the novel a weak and prosperous class of people is supported by a subjugated class of hard working beastly people. He even travels 30,000,000 years into the future to find it devoid of humans and overrun with lichen and tentacled creatures that seem somewhat similar to the Martians featured in *The War of the Worlds*. The time traveler does so through the use of the fourth dimension which Albert Einstein substantiated in his own research on continuum of space-time.

The Island of Doctor Moreau was Wells attempt of showing the ill effects of manipulating nature. Here, Doctor Moreau transforms animals into human-like creatures that eventually take over the island and kill the doctor. As a Darwinist, Wells supported the idea of evolution and warned that humanity was not the last stage of the evolutionary chain. He wrote the novel at the time of heated debate over treatment of animals in scientific experiments.

The Invisible Man deals with scientists who tamper with nature to increase their own powers. The scientist of the novel basically sells his soul for science and discovers a way to render himself invisible. The only problem is that he cannot revert back to normal and, thus, goes insane. The novel ends with the entire town turning into a mob to capture and kill him.

The War of the Worlds was written at a time of great interest in Mars. Astronomers had claimed that the red planet was covered with canals that could be a source of water. The novel also played into the invasion literature that was popular at the time, but with a mischievous twist. Though the Martians were invading England, Wells made them technologically advanced over the British. The British Empire was at its extent at the time with their superior navy and fighting force. Natives of underdeveloped countries did not stand a chance of stopping the spread of imperialism. Likewise, in the novel, the British had no chance of stopping the tripods from taking over the planet. The British Empire was getting a taste of its own medicine. The Martians utilized areal bombings and chemical warfare to subdue the population, eerily close to the German aerial bombardment of London and their use of chemical weapons on the battle field decades later. The only thing that could defeat the Martians was disease, just as the British were suffering from many diseases in their new homes away from home.

H.G. Wells would have wanted to be remembered for his social Darwinism and efforts to bring about a world of equal class (the Nazis put him near the top of their list of intellectuals to kill once they invaded England because of his socialist views); however, his science fiction took precedence over his science, and he is now remembered as a classical science fiction writer. His later life became plagued from dissatisfaction over the way the world accepted his views. And most of his later writing was often ignored. Wells died on August 13, 1946 from unspecified reasons. Since he was a diabetic, many speculate he died from that or liver cancer.

The Remarkable Case of Davidson's Eyes

I.

The transitory[1] mental aberration[2] of Sidney Davidson, remarkable enough in itself, is still more remarkable if Wade's explanation is to be credited. It sets one dreaming of the oddest possibilities of intercommunication in the future, of spending an intercalary[3] five minutes on the other side of the world, or being watched in our most secret operations by unsuspected eyes. It happened that I was the immediate witness of Davidson's seizure, and so it falls naturally to me to put the story upon paper.

When I say that I was the immediate witness of his seizure, I mean that I was the first on the scene. The thing happened at the Harlow Technical College, just beyond the Highgate Archway.[4] He was alone in the larger laboratory when the thing happened. I was in a smaller room, where the balances are, writing up some notes. The thunderstorm had completely upset my work, of course. It was just after one of the louder peals[5] that I thought I heard some glass smash in the other room. I stopped writing, and turned round to listen. For a moment I heard nothing; the hail was playing the devil's tattoo[6] on the corrugated zinc of the

---

1. **transitory**: temporary
2. **aberration**: hallucination or lapse in mental function; dream
3. **intercalary**: additional; extra
4. **Harlow Technical College... Highgate Archway**: located in northern London, England
5. **peal**: sound; thunderclap
6. **tattoo**: rhythm; drumming sound

roof. Then came another sound, a smash—no doubt of it this time. Something heavy had been knocked off the bench. I jumped up at once and went and opened the door leading into the big laboratory.

I was surprised to hear a queer sort of laugh, and saw Davidson standing unsteadily in the middle of the room, with a dazzled look on his face. My first impression was that he was drunk. He did not notice me. He was clawing out at something invisible a yard[7] in front of his face. He put out his hand, slowly, rather hesitatingly, and then clutched nothing. "What's come to it?" he said. He held up his hands to his face, fingers spread out. "Great Scott!" he said. The thing happened three or four years ago, when everyone swore by that personage. Then he began raising his feet clumsily, as though he had expected to find them glued to the floor.

"Davidson!" cried I. "What's the matter with you?" He turned round in my direction and looked about for me. He looked over me and at me and on either side of me, without the slightest sign ot seeing me. "Waves," he said; "and a remarkably neat schooner.[8] I'd swear that was Bellow's voice. *Hullo!*" He shouted suddenly at the top of his voice.

I thought he was up to some foolery. Then I saw littered about his feet the shattered remains of the best of our electrometers. "What's up, man?" said I. "You've smashed the electrometer!"

"Bellows again!" said he. "Friends left, if my hands are gone. Something about electrometers. Which way *are* you, Bellows?" He suddenly came staggering towards me. "The damned stuff cuts like butter," he said. He walked straight into the bench

7. **yard**: a type of measurement equal to .9144 meters

8. **schooner**: a type of sailing vessel that has at least two masts

and recoiled. "None so buttery that!" he said, and stood swaying.

I felt scared. "Davidson," said I, "what on earth's come over you?"

He looked round him in every direction. "I could swear that was Bellows. Why don't you show yourself like a man, Bellows?"

It occurred to me that he must be suddenly struck blind. I walked round the table and laid my hand upon his arm. I never saw a man more startled in my life. He jumped away from me, and came round into an attitude of self-defense, his face fairly distorted with terror. "Good God!" he cried. "What was that?"

"It's I—Bellows. Confound it, Davidson!"

He jumped when I answered him and stared—how can I express it?—right through me. He began talking, not to me, but to himself. "Here in broad daylight on a clear beach. Not a place to hide in." He looked about him wildly. "Here! I'm *off*." He suddenly turned and ran headlong into the big electro-magnet—so violently that, as we found afterwards, he bruised his shoulder and jawbone cruelly. At that he stepped back a pace, and cried out with almost a whimper, "What, in Heaven's name, has come over me?" He stood, blanched with terror and trembling violently, with his right arm clutching his left, where that had collided with the magnet.

By that time I was excited and fairly scared. "Davidson," said I, "don't be afraid."

He was startled at my voice, but not so excessively as before. I repeated my words in as clear and as firm a tone as I could assume. "Bellows," he said, "is that you?"

"Cant you see it's me?"

He laughed. "I can't even see it's myself. Where the devil are we?"

"Here," said I, "in the laboratory."

"The laboratory!" he answered in a puzzled tone, and put his hand to his forehead. "I *was* in the laboratory—till that flash came, but I'm hanged[9] if I'm there now. What ship is that?"

"There's no ship," said I. "Do be sensible, old chap.[10]"

"No ship!" he repeated, and seemed to forget my denial forthwith. "I suppose," said he slowly, "we're both dead. But the rummy[11] part is I feel just as though I still had a body. Don't get used to it all at once, I suppose. The old shop was struck by lightning, I suppose. Jolly[12] quick thing, Bellows—eigh?"[13]

"Don't talk nonsense. You're very much alive. You are in the laboratory, blundering about. You've just smashed a new electrometer. I don t envy you when Boyce arrives."

He stared away from me towards the diagrams of cryohydrates.[14] "I must be deaf,"said he. "They've fired a gun, for there goes the puff of smoke, and I never heard a sound."

I put my hand on his arm again, and this time he was less alarmed. "We seem to have a sort of invisible bodies," said he. "By Jove![15] there's a boat coming round the headland. It's very much like the old life after all—in a different climate."

I shook his arm. "Davidson," I cried, "wake up!"

---

9. **be hanged**: (British) colloquial expression of concern or anxiety; similar to cursing
10. **old chap**: (British) colloquial expression meaning "friend"
11. **rummy**: strange
12. **jolly**: (British) colloquial adjective meaning "great" or "thorough"
13. **eigh**: used to voice exclamation
14. **cryohydrates**: solids that form at the lowest temperature possible for solidification
15. **By Jove!**: (British) colloquial expression to voice surprise

II.

It was just then that Boyce came in. So soon as he spoke Davidson exclaimed: "Old Boyce! Dead too! What a lark!"[16] I hastened to explain that Davidson was in a kind of somnambulistic[17] trance. Boyce was interested at once. We both did all we could to rouse the fellow out of his extraordinary state. He answered our questions, and asked us some of his own, but his attention seemed distracted by his hallucination about a beach and a ship. He kept interpolating[18] observations concerning some boat and the davits,[19] and sails filling with the wind. It made one feel queer, in the dusky laboratory, to hear him saying such things.

He was blind and helpless. We had to walk him down the passage, one at each elbow, to Boyce's private room, and while Boyce talked to him there, and humoured him about this ship idea, I went along the corridor and asked old Wade to come and look at him. The voice of our Dean sobered him a little, but not very much. He asked where his hands were, and why he had to walk about up to his waist in the ground. Wade thought over him a long time—you know how he knits his brows—and then made him feel the couch, guiding his hands to it. "That's a couch," said Wade. "The couch in the private room of Professor Boyce. Horse-hair stuffing."

Davidson felt about, and puzzled over it, and answered presently that he could feel it all right, but he couldn't see it.

---

16. **What a lark**: Colloquial expression meaning "how amusing"
17. **somnambulistic**: sleepwalking
18. **interpolate**: introduce new ideas into a conversation
19. **davit**: a crane rising off the side of a boat

"What *do* you see?" asked Wade. Davidson said he could see nothing but a lot of sand and broken-up shells. Wade gave him some other things to feel, telling him what they were, and watching him keenly.

"The ship is almost hull[20] down," said Davidson presently, *apropos* of[21] nothing.

"Never mind the ship," said Wade. "Listen to me, Davidson. Do you know what hallucination means?"

"Rather," said Davidson.

"Well, everything you see is hallucinatory."

"Bishop Berkeley,"[22] said Davidson.

"Don't mistake me," said Wade. "You are alive and in this room of Boyce's. But something has happened to your eyes. You cannot see; you can feel and hear, but not see. Do you follow me?"

"It seems to me that I see too much." Davidson rubbed his knuckles into his eyes. "Well?" he said.

"That's all. Don't let it perplex you. Bellows here and I will take you home in a cab."

"Wait a bit." Davidson thought. "Help me to sit down," said he presently; "and now—I'm sorry to trouble you—but will you tell me all that over again?"

Wade repeated it very patiently. Davidson shut his eyes, and pressed his hands upon his forehead. "Yes," said he. "It's quite right. Now my eyes are shut I know you're right. That's you, Bellows, sitting by me on the couch. I'm in England again. And we're in the dark."

---

20. **hull**: the bottom, hollow part of a ship
21. **apropos of**: in regard to; in reference to
22. **Bishop Berkeley**: (1685-1753) Irish philosopher who said, "To be is to be perceived."

Then he opened his eyes. "And there," said he, "is the sun just rising, and the yards of the ship, and a tumbled sea, and a couple of birds flying. I never saw anything so real. And I'm sitting up to my neck in a bank of sand."

He bent forward and covered his face with his hands. Then he opened his eyes again. "Dark sea and sunrise! And yet I'm sitting on a sofa in old Boyce's room!... God help me!"

III.

That was the beginning. For three weeks this strange affection[23] of Davidson's eyes continued unabated. It was far worse than being blind. He was absolutely helpless, and had to be fed like a newly-hatched bird, and led about and undressed. If he attempted to move, he fell over things or struck himself against walls or doors. After a day or so he got used to hearing our voices without seeing us, and willingly admitted he was at home, and that Wade was right in what he told him. My sister, to whom he was engaged, insisted on coming to see him, and would sit for hours every day while he talked about this beach of his. Holding her hand seemed to comfort him immensely. He explained that when we left the College and drove home—he lived in Hampstead village[24]—it appeared to him as if we drove right through a sandhill—it was perfectly black until he emerged again—and through rocks and trees and solid obstacles, and when he was taken to his own room it made him giddy and almost frantic with the fear of falling, because going upstairs

23. **affection**: condition

24. **Hampstead village**: a village that is now part of greater London

seemed to lift him thirty or forty feet above the rocks of his imaginary island. He kept saying he should smash all the eggs. The end was that he had to be taken down into his father's consulting room and laid upon a couch that stood there.

He described the island as being a bleak kind of place on the whole, with very little vegetation, except some peaty stuff, and a lot of bare rock. There were multitudes of penguins, and they made the rocks white and disagreeable to see. The sea was often rough, and once there was a thunderstorm, and he lay and shouted at the silent flashes. Once or twice seals pulled up on the beach, but only on the first two or three days. He said it was very funny the way in which the penguins used to waddle right through him, and how he seemed to lie among them without disturbing them.

I remember one odd thing, and that was when he wanted very badly to smoke. We put a pipe in his hands—he almost poked his eye out with it—and lit it. But he couldn't taste anything. I've since found it's the same with me—I don't know if it's the usual case—that I cannot enjoy tobacco at all unless I can see the smoke.

But the queerest part of his vision came when Wade sent him out in a Bath-chair[25] to get fresh air. The Davidsons hired a chair, and got that deaf and obstinate dependant of theirs, Widgery, to attend to it. Widgery's ideas of healthy expeditions were peculiar. My sister, who had been to the Dogs' Home,[26] met them in Camden Town,[27] towards King's Cross,[28] Widgery trotting

25. **Bath-chair**: a old fashioned wheelchair; was first developed in Bath, England
26. **Dog's Home**: a shelter for battered dogs and cats located in Battersea, an old village along the Thames, now located in greater London
27. **Camden Town**: an inner-city market district in North London,

along complacently, and Davidson, evidently most distressed, trying in his feeble, blind way to attract Widgery's attention.

He positively wept when my sister spoke to him. "Oh, get me out of this horrible darkness!" he said, feeling for her hand. "I must get out of it, or I shall die." He was quite incapable of explaining what was the matter, but my sister decided he must go home, and presently, as they went uphill towards Hampstead, the horror seemed to drop from him. He said it was good to see the stars again, though it was then about noon and a blazing day.

"It seemed," he told me afterwards, "as if I was being carried irresistibly towards the water. I was not very much alarmed at first. Of course it was night there—a lovely night."

"Of course?" I asked, for that struck me as odd.

"Of course," said he. "It's always night there when it is day here... Well, we went right into the water, which was calm and shining under the moonlight—just a broad swell that seemed to grow broader and flatter as I came down into it. The surface glistened just like a skin—it might have been empty space underneath for all I could tell to the contrary. Very slowly, for I rode slanting into it, the water crept up to my eyes. Then I went under and the skin seemed to break and heal again about my eyes. The moon gave a jump up in the sky and grew green and dim, and fish, faintly glowing, came darting round me—and things that seemed made of luminous glass; and I passed through a tangle of seaweeds that shone with an oily lustre. And so I drove down into the sea, and the stars went out one by one, and the moon grew greener and darker, and the seaweed became a luminous purple-red. It was all very faint and mysterious, and everything seemed to quiver. And all the while I could hear the wheels of

---

28. King's Cross: a district in the inner-city of London with a railroad station

the Bath-chair creaking, and the footsteps of people going by, and a man in the distance selling the special *Pall Mall*.[29]

"I kept sinking down deeper and deeper into the water. It became inky black about me, not a ray from above came down into that darkness, and the phosphorescent[30] things grew brighter and brighter. The snaky branches of the deeper weeds flickered like the flames of spirit-lamps; but, after a time, there were no more weeds. The fishes came staring and gaping towards me, and into me and through me. I never imagined such fishes before. They had lines of fire along the sides of them as though they had been outlined with a luminous pencil. And there was a ghastly thing swimming backwards with a lot of twining arms.[31] And then I saw, coming very slowly towards me through the gloom, a hazy mass of light that resolved itself as it drew nearer into multitudes of fishes, struggling and darting round something that drifted. I drove on straight towards it, and presently I saw in the midst of the tumult, and by the light of the fish, a bit of splintered spar[32] looming over me, and a dark hull tilting over, and some glowing phosphorescent forms that were shaken and writhed as the fish bit at them. Then it was I began to try to attract Widgery's attention. A horror came upon me. Ugh! I should have driven right into those half-eaten—things. If your sister had not come! They had great holes in them, Bellows, and ... Never mind. But it was ghastly!"

---

29. *Pall Mall*: an evening London newspaper, which published many of H.G. Wells' stories, this one including
30. **phosphorescent**: luminous; glowing
31. **ghastly thing ... twining arms**: probably a reference to a squid and how it swims
32. **spar**: a mast to hold up sails

IV.

For three weeks Davidson remained in this singular state, seeing what at the time we imagined was an altogether phantasmal world, and stone blind to the world around him. Then, one Tuesday, when I called I met old Davidson in the passage. "He can see his thumb!" the old gentleman said, in a perfect transport. He was struggling into his overcoat. "He can see his thumb, Bellows!" he said, with the tears in his eyes. "The lad will be all right yet."

I rushed in to Davidson. He was holding up a little book before his face, and looking at it and laughing in a weak kind of way.

"It's amazing," said he. "There's a kind of patch come there." He pointed with his finger. "I'm on the rocks as usual, and the penguins are staggering and flapping about as usual, and there's been a whale showing every now and then, but it's got too dark now to make him out. But put something *there,* and I see it—I do see it. It's very dim and broken in places, but I see it all the same, like a faint spectre of itself. I found it out this morning while they were dressing me. It's like a hole in this infernal phantom world. Just put your hand by mine. No—not there. Ah! Yes! I see it. The base of your thumb and a bit of cuff! It looks like the ghost of a bit of your hand sticking out of the darkling sky. Just by it there's a group of stars like a cross coming out.[33]"

From that time Davidson began to mend. His account of the change, like his account of the vision, was oddly convincing. Over

---

33. **stars like a cross coming out**: the Southern Cross constellation; also known as the Crux; a group of stars visible mostly in the Southern Hemisphere

patches of his field of vision, the phantom world grew fainter, grew transparent, as it were, and through these translucent gaps he began to see dimly the real world about him. The patches grew in size and number, ran together and spread until only here and there were blind spots left upon his eyes. He was able to get up and steer himself about, feed himself once more, read, smoke, and behave like an ordinary citizen again. At first it was very confusing to him to have these two pictures overlapping each other like the changing views of a lantern, but in a little while he began to distinguish the real from the illusory.

At first he was unfeignedly[34] glad, and seemed only too anxious to complete his cure by taking exercise and tonics. But as that odd island of his began to fade away from him, he became queerly interested in it. He wanted particularly to go down into the deep sea again, and would spend half his time wandering about the low-lying parts of London, trying to find the water-logged wreck he had seen drifting. The glare of real daylight very soon impressed him so vividly as to blot out everything of his shadowy world, but of a night-time, in a darkened room, he could still see the white-splashed rocks of the island, and the clumsy penguins staggering to and fro. But even these grew fainter and fainter, and, at last, soon after he married my sister, he saw them for the last time.

V.

And now to tell of the queerest thing of all. About two years after his cure I dined with the Davidsons, and after dinner a man named Atkins called in. He is a lieutenant in the Royal

34. **unfeignedly**: sincerely

Navy, and a pleasant, talkative man. He was on friendly terms with my brother-in-law, and was soon on friendly terms with me. It came out that he was engaged to Davidson's cousin, and incidentally he took out a kind of pocket photograph case to show us a new rendering of his *fiancée.* "And, by-the-by," said he, "here's the old *Fulmar.*"[35]

Davidson looked at it casually. Then suddenly his face lit up. "Good heavens!" said he. "I could almost swear—"

"What?" said Atkins.

"That I had seen that ship before."

"Don't see how you can have. She hasn't been out of the South Seas for six years, and before then——"

"But," began Davidson, and then, "Yes—that's the ship I dreamt of; I'm sure that's the ship I dreamt of. She was standing off an island that swarmed with penguins, and she fired a gun."

"Good Lord!" said Atkins, who had now heard the particulars of the seizure. "How the deuce[36] could you dream that?"

And then, bit by bit, it came out that on the very day Davidson was seized, H.M.S.[37] *Fulmar* had actually been off a little rock to the south of Antipodes Island.[38] A boat had landed overnight to get penguins' eggs, had been delayed, and a thunderstorm drifting up, the boat's crew had waited until the morning before rejoining the ship. Atkins had been one of them, and he corroborated, word for word, the descriptions Davidson had given of the island and the boat. There is not the slightest doubt

35. *Fulmar*: a British navy ship

36. **deuce**: the devil; "how the deuce" is a form of cursing

37. **H.M.S.**: acronym for Her Majesty's Ship; a prefix attached to all Royal Navy ships

38. **Antipodes Island**: an uninhabited island south of New Zealand

in any of our minds that Davidson has really seen the place. In some unaccountable way, while he moved hither and thither in London, his sight moved hither and thither in a manner that corresponded, about this distant island. *How* is absolutely a mystery.

That completes the remarkable story of Davidson's eyes. It's perhaps the best authenticated case in existence of real vision at a distance. Explanation there is none forthcoming, except what Professor Wade has thrown out. But his explanation invokes the Fourth Dimension,[39] and a dissertation on theoretical kinds of space. To talk of there being "a kink in space" seems mere nonsense to me; it may be because I am no mathematician. When I said that nothing would alter the fact that the place is eight thousand miles away, he answered that two points might be a yard away on a sheet of paper, and yet be brought together by bending the paper round. The reader may grasp his argument, but I certainly do not. His idea seems to be that Davidson, stooping between the poles of the big electro-magnet, had some extraordinary twist given to his retinal elements through the sudden change in the field of force due to the lightning.

He thinks, as a consequence of this, that it may be possible to live visually in one part of the world, while one lives bodily in another. He has even made some experiments in support of his views; but, so far, he has simply succeeded in blinding a few dogs. I believe that is the net result of his work, though I have not seen him for some weeks. Latterly I have been so busy with my work in connection with the Saint Pancras installation[40] that I have had little opportunity of calling to see him. But the whole

---

39. **Fourth Dimension**: a plane beyond normal human experience
40. **Saint Pancras installation**: a probable reference to the Saint Pancras railway station opened in 1868

of his theory seems fantastic to me. The facts concerning Davidson stand on an altogether different footing, and I can testify personally to the accuracy of every detail I have given.

Commentary

The case of Davidson's eyes is curious indeed. H.G. Wells' account of how a man exists in two places on opposite sides of the world simultaneously is both captivating and horrifying in its realism. If readers did not know any better, they could feel that this story has a shocking sense of credibility to it, as if it could have really happened. It is not the science of this story that captivates the readers, it is too vague and fantastical, but it is the philosophy that resonates. It is familiar as it is strange. With a mention of one name, Bishop Berkeley, the reason is made clear. Wells is not telling a new story, rather an old story in a new way.

The narrator Bellows, along with the reader, stumbles upon Davidson in a fugue state, flailing blindly around his laboratory, crashing into all the equipment. Davidson seems delusional, hearing vaguely what the narrator is saying without being able to see him, and babbling on about beaches and boats. Through their conversation, the sense that Davidson's perception of sight is seriously put off is made clearer when he talks about seeing things but not hearing them. " 'I must be deaf,' said he. 'They've fired a gun, for there goes the puff of smoke, and I never heard a sound.' " He has sight sense in one area, and obviously the other four senses in another. But how can this be? Is it really so spectacular to believe? Not according to certain philosophers, especially Bishop George Berkeley.

Wade, the Dean of their department, thinks he has stumbled upon Davidson's problem. "Well, everything you see is hallucinatory," he says, referring to the perception of every person in the world. In other words, it is not out of the ordinary to be fooled by any of the five senses. In fact, as most philosophers feel, the real world is but a shadow of another world of ideals. Davidson catches on right away and mentions Bishop Berkeley, who was an Irish bishop and empiricist. As an empiricist, Berkeley believed that the world could only be known through the five senses of sight, sound, taste, touch, and smell. In other words, to assume that anything exists outside of the five senses is jumping to faulty conclusions. Berkeley postulated that the material world is only perceived through the human mind, which has no limits in time or space, being eternal as the creator of the mind is eternal, yet humans can only perceive a fraction of such infinite possibilities. What has happened to Davidson is that he is able to suddenly see objects on the opposite end of the world. What Berkeley would postulate is that the distance between Davidson and the island is irrelevant, since the finite mind only understands distance experienced in the past in relation to what is seen and touched. A tree seen two centimeters away and a tree viewed two kilometers away look completely different, though it is the same tree. The only difference is that the sight perception of the tree has changed through physical movement. Now what if the perception of sight is no longer needed to physically be moved, but the distance "twisted" to bring the perception of the object closer?

Bellows mentions Professor Wade speculating on the Fourth Dimension where "a kink in space" has been produced. At the time of H.G. Wells this type of speculative mathematics was obscure; however, with the popularization of science fiction, it is almost a staple of the genre. In order to grasp a twist in space itself, the Möbius strip, discovered in part by the German mathematician August Möbius, needs to be understood. A Möbius strip is basically a strip of paper twisted 180 degrees with the two ends then glued together. Though the strip has two sides, a side A and a side B when flat, twisted into a Möbius strip there is only one side. Thus, a person standing on such a strip could walk around the whole strip and encounter both side A and side B of the strip. Now, before creating "a kink in space," lay a long strip of paper strip with side A facing up, and write Davidson at the top of the strip. Then at the bottom of the strip write South Pacific island. Both Davidson and the South Pacific island should be at opposites ends of each other and at the greatest distance. Then twist the strip 180 degrees and glue the two ends together. What happens is that both Davidson and the South Pacific island pieces now touch each other. With the aid of the electro-magnet, Davidson's perception of sight is what is twisted; thus, he is able to exist in London, while his sight perceives the South Pacific on the opposite side of the world. If this is not a physical phenomenon then it could easily be attributed to light bending along the strip so that, though his eyes are physically in London, he can actually perceive the South Pacific island.

Continental Short Stories

Guy de Maupassant (France): The Diamond Necklace (1884)
Franz Kafka (Germany): The Country Doctor (1919)

Introduction of the Author

Guy De Maupassant (1850-1893)

Considered the greatest French short story writer, Guy De Maupassant is most famous for his naturalistic style of writing and as the father of the modern short story. Maupassant was born of affluent parents and, when his mother was in her youth, she was even playmates with Gustave Flaubert (1821-1880), who later became most famous for his novel *Madam Bovary* (1857). His mother had great literary tastes, and having known the great Flaubert, Maupassant chose to stay with his mother when his parents divorced. In his late teens he even had the opportunity to meet Flaubert, who later became his mentor and had a great influence on his writing. Maupassant continued his schooling, and though he may have had a rebellious streak, he aimed to become a scholar, showing greater interest in poetry and theater. However, with the breakout to the Franco-Prussian war (1870-1871), he volunteered to fight for his country, yet his rebellious streak continued, and the army was forced to discipline him on several occasions. Upon the end of the war, when France lost most of its empire, Maupassant settled in Paris where he worked as a clerk for the Navy. There, he may have dwindled into obscurity if not for his literary hero, Flaubert.

Making him his protégé, Flaubert helped Maupassant break into journalism and even invited him into his literary circle that included the likes of Henry James and Emile Zola. By 1880, Maupassant had published his first short story that is arguably his best, "*Boule de Souif*," which takes place during the Franco

-Prussian war. *Boule de Souif,* literally translated as 'ball of fat,' is the name of a nationalistic prostitute who flees with nine other refugees by stage coach from their town now occupied by the Prussians. He used the story to contrast the amorality of the middle class with the patriotism of a lower class prostitute. This story was one of many in a collected volume, and with the success of the story, he followed his acclaim by writing prolifically three to four volumes of short stories a year. In a ten year period, he had written around 300 short stories. At the same time he wrote short stories, he even wrote six novels, his first being *A Woman's Life* (*Une Vie,* 1883). Though his writing was popular, Maupassant avoided society life and took great joy in voyaging around Europe and Africa in his private yacht. After each voyage, he would have a new volume of stories to sell.

Maupassant's stories have been labeled naturalistic in that they imitate or represent what is real as opposed to romantic that stresses the fanciful or unreal. The naturalistic school, which Flaubert championed at its early stages and Maupassant reveled in, started in France as a direct reaction to the Romantic Movement. Realist literature centered on the middle class by depicting events and their consequences with as little bias on the writers part as possible. A good example is "The Diamond Necklace," which has a middle class couple suffer the indignity of having to scrounge and save to pay for a borrowed jewel necklace they have lost, only to find out that the necklace was a worthless fake. Such social issues as social equality, justice, unemployment, and poverty play important roles in the naturalistic school, where "The Diamond Necklace" places emphasis on over reaching one's goals for superficial ideals. Even his thirty-nine horror stories, though closely resembling Edgar Allan Poe's style of romantic psychological horror, detail the downward spiral of the protagonists into madness that was often the result of a troubled mind more than outside forces. With such range to his stories, Maupassant's horror fiction has been likened to Edgar Allan Poe and has influenced many writers after him, including horror writer H.P. Lovecraft, master story teller O. Henry, who uses a similar style with twist endings, and playwright Anton Chekhov.

Maupassant's idea of the modern novel was not to aim at "telling a story or entertaining us or touching our hearts but at forcing us to think and understand the deeper, hidden meaning of events." This statement takes on a rather ironic twist; as his stories are want to do, when he wrote a rather effective horror short story called "*Le Horla*" (1887). The Horla (from French "*Hors*", outside and "*de la*", there) are strange beings that cannot be seen and cousins to the vampire, but the narrator senses one of them coming off of a ghost ship. It eventually drives him mad, and he commits suicide to rid himself of it. In the early 1870's, Maupassant had contracted syphilis, which causes mental disorders. As his dementia grew worse, so did his paranoia of persecution. Many critics feel that "*Le Horla*" was actually written under the sickness of dementia and has a type of autobiographical sensibility to it. His never ending quest for isolation from fame led him to ultimately slit his own throat. He was committed to an asylum where he eventually died on July 6, 1893, six years after writing "*Le Horla.*"

The Diamond Necklace

The girl was one of those pretty and charming young creatures who sometimes are born, as if by a slip of fate, into a family of clerks. She had no dowry,[1] no expectations, no way of being known, understood, loved, married by any rich and distinguished man; so she let herself be married to a little clerk of the Ministry of Public Instruction.

She dressed plainly because she could not dress well, but she was unhappy as if she had really fallen from a higher station; since with women there is neither caste nor rank, for beauty, grace and charm take the place of family and birth. Natural ingenuity,[2] instinct for what is elegant, a supple[3] mind are their sole hierarchy, and often make of women of the people the equals of the very greatest ladies.

Mathilde suffered ceaselessly, feeling herself born to enjoy all delicacies and all luxuries. She was distressed at the poverty of her dwelling, at the bareness of the walls, at the shabby chairs, the ugliness of the curtains. All those things, of which another woman of her rank would never even have been conscious, tortured her and made her angry. The sight of the little Breton[4] peasant who did her humble housework aroused in her despairing regrets and bewildering dreams. She thought of silent antechambers hung with Oriental tapestry, illumined by tall bronze

---

1. **dowry**: money the bride's family saves to give to the groom's family
2. **ingenuity**: imagination
3. **supple**: flexible
4. **Breton**: a person from Brittany, a peninsula on the northwest tip of France

candelabra, and of two great footmen in knee breeches who sleep in the big armchairs, made drowsy by the oppressive heat of the stove. She thought of long reception halls hung with ancient silk, of the dainty cabinets containing priceless curiosities and of the little coquettish[5] perfumed reception rooms made for chatting at five o'clock with intimate friends, with men famous and sought after, whom all women envy and whose attention they all desire.

When she sat down to dinner, before the round table covered with a tablecloth in use three days, opposite her husband, who uncovered the soup tureen[6] and declared with a delighted air, "Ah, the good soup! I don't know anything better than that," she thought of dainty dinners, of shining silverware, of tapestry that peopled the walls with ancient personages and with strange birds flying in the midst of a fairy forest; and she thought of delicious dishes served on marvelous plates and of the whispered gallantries to which you listen with a sphinx-like[7] smile while you are eating the pink meat of a trout or the wings of a quail.[8]

She had no gowns, no jewels, nothing. And she loved nothing but that. She felt made for that. She would have liked so much to please, to be envied, to be charming, to be sought after.

She had a friend, a former schoolmate at the convent, who was rich, and whom she did not like to go to see any more because she felt so sad when she came home.

But one evening her husband reached home with a triumphant air and holding a large envelope in his hand.

---

5. **coquettish**: flirtatious
6. **tureen**: a large, deep bowl used for serving soup
7. **sphinx-like**: mysterious or inscrutable
8. **quail**: a small game bird whose meat was as popular to eat as chicken

"There," said he, "there is something for you."

She tore the paper quickly and drew out a printed card which bore these words:

> The Minister of Public Instruction and Madame Georges Ramponneau request the honor of M. and Madame Loisel's company at the palace of the Ministry on Monday evening, January 18th.

Instead of being delighted, as her husband had hoped, she threw the invitation on the table crossly, muttering:

"What do you wish me to do with that?"

"Why, my dear, I thought you would be glad. You never go out, and this is such a fine opportunity. I had great trouble to get it. Everyone wants to go; it is very select, and they are not giving many invitations to clerks. The whole official world will be there."

She looked at him with an irritated glance and said impatiently:

"And what do you wish me to put on my back?"

He had not thought of that. He stammered:

"Why, the gown you go to the theatre in. It looks very well to me."He stopped, distracted, seeing that his wife was weeping. Two great tears ran slowly from the corners of her eyes toward the corners of her mouth.

"What's the matter? What's the matter?" he answered.

By a violent effort she conquered her grief and replied in a calm voice, while she wiped her wet cheeks:

"Nothing. Only I have no gown, and, therefore, I can't go to this ball. Give your card to some colleague whose wife is better equipped than I am."

He was in despair. He resumed:

"Come, let us see, Mathilde. How much would it cost, a suitable gown, which you could use on other occasions—something very simple?"

She reflected several seconds, making her calculations and wondering also what sum she could ask without drawing on herself an immediate refusal and a frightened exclamation from the economical clerk.

Finally she replied hesitating:

"I don't know exactly, but I think I could manage it with four hundred francs.[9]"

He grew a little pale, because he was laying aside just that amount to buy a gun and treat himself to a little shooting next summer on the plain of Nanterre,[10] with several friends who went to shoot larks[11] there of a Sunday.

But he said:

"Very well. I will give you four hundred francs. And try to have a pretty gown."

The day of the ball drew near and Madame Loisel seemed sad, uneasy, anxious. Her frock was ready, however. Her husband said to her one evening:

"What is the matter? Come, you have seemed very queer[12] these last three days."

And she answered:

"It annoys me not to have a single piece of jewelry, not a

---

9. **four hundred francs**: inflation and exchange adjusted to be about $2,072.54 (a rough estimate of what the 19th century franc was worth compared to the 19th century dollar = .193 French francs=1 American dollar)

10. **Nanterre**: a commune in northern France, now a western suburb of Paris

11. **lark**: a small singing bird, popular sport for shooting

12. **queer**: strange or odd

single ornament, nothing to put on. I shall look poverty-stricken. I would almost rather not go at all."

"You might wear natural flowers," said her husband. "They're very stylish at this time of year. For ten francs[13] you can get two or three magnificent roses."

She was not convinced.

"No; there's nothing more humiliating than to look poor among other women who are rich."

"How stupid you are!" her husband cried. "Go look up your friend, Madame Forestier, and ask her to lend you some jewels. You're intimate enough with her to do that."

She uttered a cry of joy:

"True! I never thought of it."

The next day she went to her friend and told her of her distress.

Madame Forestier went to a wardrobe with a mirror, took out a large jewel box, brought it back, opened it and said to Madame Loisel:

"Choose, my dear."

She saw first some bracelets, then a pearl necklace, then a Venetian gold cross set with precious stones, of admirable workmanship. She tried on the ornaments before the mirror, hesitated and could not make up her mind to part with them, to give them back. She kept asking:

"Haven't you anymore?"

"Why, yes. Look further; I don't know what you like."

Suddenly she discovered, in a black satin box, a superb diamond necklace, and her heart throbbed with an immoderate[14]

---

13. **ten francs**: inflation and exchange adjusted to be about $51.81

14. **immoderate**: excessive

desire. Her hands trembled as she took it. She fastened it round her throat, outside her high-necked waist, and was lost in ecstasy at her reflection in the mirror.

Then she asked, hesitating, filled with anxious doubt:

"Will you lend me this, only this?"

"Why, yes, certainly."

She threw her arms round her friend's neck, kissed her passionately, then fled with her treasure.

The night of the ball arrived. Madame Loisel was a great success. She was prettier than any other woman present, elegant, graceful, smiling and wild with joy. All the men looked at her, asked her name, sought to be introduced. All the attachés[15] of the Cabinet wished to waltz with her. She was remarked by the minister himself.

She danced with rapture, with passion, intoxicated by pleasure, forgetting all in the triumph of her beauty, in the glory of her success, in a sort of cloud of happiness comprised of all this homage,[16] admiration, these awakened desires and of that sense of triumph which is so sweet to woman's heart.

She left the ball about four o'clock in the morning. Her husband had been sleeping since midnight in a little deserted anteroom with three other gentlemen whose wives were enjoying the ball.

He threw over her shoulders the wraps he had brought, the modest wraps of common life, the poverty of which contrasted with the elegance of the ball dress. She felt this and wished to escape so as not to be remarked by the other women, who were enveloping themselves in costly furs.

---

15. **attaché**: a person attached to the legislature or embassy
16. **homage**: respect

Loisel held her back, saying: "Wait a bit. You will catch cold outside. I will call a cab."

But she did not listen to him and rapidly descended the stairs. When they reached the street they could not find a carriage and began to look for one, shouting after the cabmen passing at a distance.

They went toward the Seine[17] in despair, shivering with cold. At last they found on the quay[18] one of those ancient night cabs which, as though they were ashamed to show their shabbiness during the day, are never seen round Paris until after dark.

It took them to their dwelling in the Rue des Martyrs,[19] and sadly they mounted the stairs to their flat. All was ended for her. As to him, he reflected that he must be at the ministry at ten o'clock that morning.

She removed her wraps before the glass so as to see herself once more in all her glory. But suddenly she uttered a cry. She no longer had the necklace around her neck!

"What is the matter with you?" demanded her husband, already half undressed.

She turned distractedly toward him.

"I have—I have—I've lost Madame Forestier's necklace," she cried.

He stood up, bewildered.

"What!—how? Impossible!"

They looked among the folds of her skirt, of her cloak, in her pockets, everywhere, but did not find it.

---

17. **Seine**: a river that flows northwest through Paris and drains into the English Channel
18. **quay**: a landing place for boats; a wharf
19. **Rue des Martyrs**: (translated: Street of Martyrs) a street located in northern Paris

"You're sure you had it on when you left the ball?" he asked.

"Yes, I felt it in the vestibule[20] of the minister's house."

"But if you had lost it in the street we should have heard it fall. It must be in the cab."

"Yes, probably. Did you take his number?"

"No. And you—didn't you notice it?"

"No."

They looked, thunderstruck, at each other. At last Loisel put on his clothes.

"I shall go back on foot," said he, "over the whole route, to see whether I can find it."

He went out. She sat waiting on a chair in her ball dress, without strength to go to bed, overwhelmed, without any fire, without a thought.

Her husband returned about seven o'clock. He had found nothing.

He went to police headquarters, to the newspaper offices to offer a reward; he went to the cab companies—everywhere, in fact, whither he was urged by the least spark of hope.

She waited all day, in the same condition of mad fear before this terrible calamity.

Loisel returned at night with a hollow, pale face. He had discovered nothing.

"You must write to your friend," said he, "that you have broken the clasp of her necklace and that you are having it mended. That will give us time to turn round."

She wrote at his dictation.

At the end of a week they had lost all hope. Loisel, who had aged five years, declared:

---

20. **vestibule**: an antechamber between the door and the interior of the house

"We must consider how to replace that ornament."

The next day they took the box that had contained it and went to the jeweler whose name was found within. He consulted his books.

"It was not I, Madame, who sold that necklace; I must simply have furnished the case."

Then they went from jeweler to jeweler, searching for a necklace like the other, trying to recall it, both sick with chagrin[21] and grief.

They found, in a shop at the Palais Royal,[22] a string of diamonds that seemed to them exactly like the one they had lost. It was worth forty thousand francs.[23] They could have it for thirty-six.

So they begged the jeweler not to sell it for three days yet. And they made a bargain that he should buy it back for thirty-four thousand francs,[24] in case they should find the lost necklace before the end of February.

Loisel possessed eighteen thousand francs[25] which his father had left him. He would borrow the rest.

He did borrow, asking a thousand francs of one, five hundred of another, five louis[26] here, three louis there. He gave notes,

---

21. **chagrin**: disappointment
22. **Palais Royal**: an old palace and garden area that, in Maupassant's time, had a popular boulevard of cafés and theaters; currently located across the street from the Louvre
23. **forty thousand francs**: $207,253.89
24. **thirty-four thousand francs**: inflation and exchange adjusted to be about $176,165.80
25. **eighteen thousand francs**: inflation and exchange adjusted to be about $93,264.25
26. **louis**: a coin similar in value to the franc; introduced by Louis XIII in 1640 that bore his likeness (replaced again in 1795 by the franc)

took up ruinous obligations, dealt with usurers[27] and all the race of lenders. He compromised all the rest of his life, risked signing a note without even knowing whether he could meet it; and, frightened by the trouble yet to come, by the black misery that was about to fall upon him, by the prospect of all the physical privations[28] and moral tortures that he was to suffer, he went to get the new necklace, laying upon the jeweler's counter thirty-six thousand francs.

When Madame Loisel took back the necklace Madame Forestier said to her with a chilly manner:

"You should have returned it sooner; I might have needed it."

She did not open the case, as her friend had so much feared. If she had detected the substitution, what would she have thought, what would she have said? Would she not have taken Madame Loisel for a thief?

Thereafter Madame Loisel knew the horrible existence of the needy. She bore her part, however, with sudden heroism. That dreadful debt must be paid. She would pay it. They dismissed their servant; they changed their lodgings; they rented a garret under the roof.

She came to know what heavy housework meant and the odious[29] cares of the kitchen. She washed the dishes, using her dainty fingers and rosy nails on greasy pots and pans. She washed the soiled linen, the shirts and the dishcloths, which she dried upon a line; she carried the slops down to the street every morning and carried up the water, stopping for breath at every landing.

---

27. **usurer**: a person who lends money with a large amount of interest; loan shark (modern usage)
28. **privation**: comfort
29. **odious**: detestable

And dressed like a woman of the people, she went to the fruiterer, the grocer, the butcher, a basket on her arm, bargaining, meeting with impertinence, defending her miserable money, sou by sou.[30]

Every month they had to meet some notes, renew others, obtain more time.

Her husband worked evenings, making up a tradesman's accounts, and late at night he often copied manuscript for five sous a page.

This life lasted ten years.

At the end of ten years they had paid everything, everything, with the rates of usury and the accumulations of the compound interest.

Madame Loisel looked old now. She had become the woman of impoverished households—strong and hard and rough. With frowsy hair, skirts askew and red hands, she talked loud while washing the floor with great swishes of water. But sometimes, when her husband was at the office, she sat down near the window and she thought of that gay evening of long ago, of that ball where she had been so beautiful and so admired.

What would have happened if she had not lost that necklace? Who knows? who knows? How strange and changeful is life! How small a thing is needed to make or ruin us!

But one Sunday, having gone to take a walk in the Champs Elysees[31] to refresh herself after the labors of the week, she suddenly perceived a woman who was leading a child. It was Madame Forestier, still young, still beautiful, still charming.

Madame Loisel felt moved. Should she speak to her? Yes, certainly. And now that she had paid, she would tell her all

---

30. **sou**: bronze coin of France; similar in value to a penny

31. **Champs Elysees**: a prestigious street in Paris with many cafés and theater

about it. Why not?

She went up.

"Good-day, Jeanne."

The other, astonished to be familiarly addressed by this plain good-wife, did not recognize her at all and stammered:

"But—Madame!—I do not know—You must have mistaken."

"No. I am Mathilde Loisel."

Her friend uttered a cry.

"Oh, my poor Mathilde! How you are changed!"

"Yes, I have had a pretty hard life, since I last saw you, and great poverty—and that because of you!"

"Of me! How so?"

"Do you remember that diamond necklace you lent me to wear at the ministerial ball?"

"Yes. Well?"

"Well, I lost it."

"What do you mean? You brought it back."

"I brought you back another exactly like it. And it has taken us ten years to pay for it. You can understand that it was not easy for us, for us who had nothing. At last it is ended, and I am very glad."

Madame Forestier had stopped.

"You say that you bought a necklace of diamonds to replace mine?"

"Yes. You never noticed it, then! They were very similar."

And she smiled with a joy that was at once proud and ingenuous.

Madame Forestier, deeply moved, took her hands.

"Oh, my poor Mathilde! Why, my necklace was paste![32] It

32. **paste**: artificial gem made of glass

was worth at most only five hundred francs!"

Commentary

When discussing "The Diamond Necklace," readers often refer to the twist ending. Though this type of ending made Maupassant famous for English readers, for not many of his stories were translated into English, it should not be the focus of the story. Instead, we, as careful readers, should concentrate on the naturalism employed by Maupassant, especially the socioeconomic determinism detailed throughout. By socioeconomic determinism, it is meant that the struggle between the classes, between the have and the have-nots, is a trap set by social and economic factors that the characters cannot avoid, or are determined to suffer through.

The tale starts off with an ironic situation where a woman of refinement and beauty, Mathilde, ends up married to a common clerk though she herself is of the same class. She feels her marriage to such a poverty stricken man has caused her to fall "from a higher station," which she has not experienced, but she dreams of living. Maupassant remains amoral and objective in the telling of this tale; he neither denounces nor commends the characters of his writing for actions that are out of their control. He does not want us, the reader, to judge the characters either, only for us to see them as ourselves. Maupassant juxtaposes the middle-class lifestyle that most in such a station are quite happy with—they have a servant, a well furnished home, and hearty meals—with the lifestyle of the aristocrats, who appear to live a life of luxury and waste. Mathilde cannot help being born beautiful and sophisticated yet poor, any more than a pig can be blamed for being born in a pig pen. A pig is not pitied for being a pig; it is pitied for living in filth and mud that its current situation has placed it in. Likewise, the reader is not to find Mathilde's situation ridiculous, only the society that she is born in.

Thus, when Mathilde goes into a temper tantrum about not having anything to wear to the Minister's ball, the reader should not be disgusted with her but with the vicious trap that all humans are caught in. This is the socioeconomic turmoil that Maupassant keeps hinting at. Human beings are nothing more than sophisticated animals, motivated by natural impulses like fear, greed, and jealousy. Malthilde, too, is driven by her basic urges and should not be hated for being human; she should just be viewed as a more rounded character. Her husband is motivated by basic impulses as well; he is motivated by selfishness. As a clerk, he has been given a tremendous opportunity to meet and greet some of the most influential people in his profession, though he will never rise in rank. It is "such a fine opportunity" where they don't give "many invitations to clerks." He has his own job and self worth to take to the ball. He even has money saved for a hunting trip with his buddies to get away from his depression. All of these opportunities identify him as a man but do not include his wife. What does she have to identify with? Mathilde, as a woman, has nothing but a natural instinct for what is elegant that "often make of women [...] the equals of the very greatest ladies." The only way she can truly fulfill her function of being a "woman" in such a society is to have jewels and clothing that express her "worth." This sense of worth, it might be mentioned, does not include her husband personally in any way, except the money he makes. She fears to look "poverty-stricken" without jewelry, which, ironically, she is not but becomes so when she loses the useless baubles.

Once the characters have been set up along with the society they live in, Maupassant next reveals the trap that is usually the source of anxiety for the have-nots: envy. Mathilde decides to borrow jewelry from Madame Forestier. Though it is not mentioned outright in the story, upon a second reading, Madame Forestier may not be as rich as she appears. If she is in possession of a fake yet "superb diamond necklace" that is placed in a "black satin box," then most of her other jewels would arguably be fake as well. Thus, she is not as well off as the Loisels think, which sets up the second ironic situation.

Mathilde tells her husband that "there's nothing more humiliating than to look poor among other women who are rich," which seems to be a fair enough assessment. Maupassant puts this maxim to the test by looking at the character and action of the forces that compel human beings to act the way they do. As Cinderella, who in taters and covered with chimney cinders, transforms temporarily to magically go to a ball where she does not belong and so implausibly falls in love with the prince, so too does Mathilde. Though this is not a romantic fairy tale, but a shockingly natural tale, she is treated as a princess at a ball: "Madame Loisel was a great success. She was prettier than any other woman present, elegant, graceful, smiling and wild with joy. All the men looked at her, asked her name, sought to be introduced. All the attaches of the Cabinet wished to waltz with her. She was remarked by the minister himself." The only difference is that upon losing her glass slipper, Cinderella is able to find it again and live happily ever after. Not so in the real world of socioeconomic forces. Mathilde loses the diamond necklace and falls into abject poverty trying to recuperate her losses. There is no handsome prince who finds it and takes her beyond her station. In fact, the loss breaks her husband financially and physically, for he "had aged five years" over night just looking for the necklace.

The tale draws to an end on a rather positive note. The Loisels spend ten years paying off their debts, and Mathilde actually has learned that she was not originally so poor after all: "hereafter Madame Loisel knew the horrible existence of the needy." For, instead of having to worry about what she wanted, she now worried about what she needed and had to work endlessly in order to achieve it. It is too bad that she cannot turn the clock back ten years and relive her life. In just a decade, "Madame Loisel looked old now." Our little Cinderella tales has actually become ironic; it has gone backwards. She started with some wealth and comfort and fallen to "become the woman of impoverished households—strong and hard and rough," who can only look back upon the past as good times without any hope of salvation.

Then she discovers the necklace was fake! The end. Maupassant leaves the tale as that. We, the reader, are left to fill in the blanks, for only the reader can understand the lesson over the pursuit of false values that will truly make a difference.

Introduction of the Author

Franz Kafka (1883-1924)

Franz Kafka was born in Prague, in what was Austria-Hungry but is now the Czech Republic, and he was named after the Polish Emperor Franz Joseph I. He had two younger brothers and three younger sisters. Though he would die before the horrors of World War II ravaged Poland, his three sisters were imprisoned in German concentration camps, and his youngest sister, Ottla, was gassed to death at Auschwitz. His father ran a fancy goods and accessories store and his mother often helped out; thus, the children were raised by governesses. Kafka never developed a close relationship with his father, who was always working and often focused his anger on his son. He became a withdrawn and quiet child who had a fondness for reading. Wishing to see his son advance in class, his father sent Kafka to German schools instead of Czech ones. Though Czech was the language of the masses, the power of the Austro-Hungry Empire ensured that German was the language of the elite. Therefore, when Kafka wrote stories, he wrote in German. His family was Jewish, but as an adult, he did not profess to follow the Jewish traditions, and most of his stories are, in fact, saturated with Christian symbolism over that of Jewish.

Kafka was a demanding student who found academic life not much to his liking. By 1901, Kafka entered university to study chemistry, which he quickly quit and changed his major to law. After a semester he changed his major again to German literature, and when he fell into constant disagreement with his professors, he changed back to law to retain his peace of mind. He wrote on and off throughout his studies, but all that he wrote was eventually destroyed. His first surviving story published was "Description of a Struggle" (1904), which took him over a year to write, and he continued to tinker with it for an additional five years. Though it is considered one of his worst stories, it actually got him noticed as an up and coming German writer. However, since he failed to garner enough fame as a writer, he could not appreciably write full time, which meant he had to take many menial jobs, such as working at insurance companies to earn money. Such jobs required long hours, and he could not focus on his writing. When he finally found an insurance job that allowed him more time to write, his father demanded he run his brother-in-law's asbestos factory in 1911, which took up all his precious time yet again. In fact, the working hours and conditions were so horrid to Kafka that he attempted suicide. The closing of the factory in 1917 literally saved his life.

In 1913, Franz was convinced by a literary friend to publish a collection of short stories in *Meditation*, and the following year he published his now famous novel *The Trial* along with a very memorable short story "The Penal Colony." Most of Kafka's stories are dark in nature, where the protagonist is helpless to fight against a corrupt system that fails to see its own corruptness. Many critics view his writing as a satirical social commentary that would not come to pass until the establishment of totalitarian regimes following the crisis of World War I. For these reasons both Nazi Germany and Communist Russia banned the reading of his books, seeing such social satire as detrimental to holding the hearts and minds of the masses.

Through his running of the asbestos factory and writing,

Kafka continued to work in insurance, and was such an asset that his superiors secured for him an exemption from the draft to fight in World War I. However, by 1917, Kafka contracted tuberculosis and became hospitalized for influenza two years later. The effects of his poor health found fruition in his writing. "A Country Doctor" was published in 1917, and reflects the darkness and insanity of an "incurable" sickness. He suffered ill health the rest of his life, and was finally admitted to a sanatorium six weeks before his death. On June 23, 1924, Franz Kafka died of tuberculosis. His will stipulated that all his written works be destroyed, but friends and family, thankfully, refused to follow his wishes and published his unfinished works posthumously, where he finally received recognition as a world class writer.

A Country Doctor[*]

I was in great difficulty. An urgent journey was facing me. A seriously ill man was waiting for me in a village ten miles distant. A severe snowstorm filled the space between him and me. I had a carriage—a light one, with large wheels, entirely suitable for our country roads. Wrapped up in furs with the bag of instruments in my hand, I was already standing in the courtyard ready for the journey; but the horse was missing—the horse. My own horse had died the previous night, as a result of over exertion in this icy winter. My servant girl was at that very moment running around the village to see if she could borrow a horse, but it was hopeless—I knew that—and I stood there useless, increasingly covered with snow, becoming all the time more immobile. The girl appeared at the gate, alone. She was swinging the lantern. Of course, who is now going to lend her his horse for such a journey? I walked once again across the courtyard. I couldn't see what to do. Distracted and tormented, I kicked my foot against the cracked door of the pigsty[1] which had not been used for years. The door opened and banged to and fro on its hinges. A warmth and smell as if from horses came out. A dim stall[2] lantern on a rope swayed inside. A man huddled down in the stall below showed his open blue-eyed face. "Shall I hitch

---

* Translated by Ian Johnston of Malaspina University-College, Nanaimo, BC, Canada, and kindly offered it in the public domain care of his website http://records.viu.ca/~johnstoi/kafka/countrydoctor.htm

1. **pigsty**: a pen for pigs
2. **stall**: a pen for horses

up?" he asked, crawling out on all fours. I didn't know what to say and bent down to see what was still in the stall. The servant girl stood beside me. "One doesn't know the sorts of things one has stored in one's own house," she said, and we both laughed. "Hey, Brother, hey Sister," the groom cried out, and two horses, powerful animals with strong flanks,[3] shoved their way one behind the other, legs close to the bodies, lowering their well-formed heads like camels, and getting through the door space, which they completely filled, only through the powerful movements of their rumps. But right away they stood up straight, long legged, with thick steaming bodies. "Help him," I said, and the girl obediently hurried to hand the wagon harnes s[4] to the groom.[5] But as soon as she was beside him, the groom put his arms around her and pushed his face against hers. She screamed out and ran over to me. On the girl's cheek were red marks from two rows of teeth. "You brute," I cried out in fury. "Do you want the whip?" But I immediately remembered that he was a stranger, that I didn't know where he came from, and that he was helping me out of his own free will, when everyone else was refusing to. As if he knew what I was thinking, he took no offence at my threat, but turned around to me once more, still busy with the horses. Then he said, "Climb in," and, in fact, everything was ready. I noticed that I have never before traveled with such a beautiful team of horses, and I climbed in happily. "But I'll take the reins. You don't know the way," I said. "Of course," he said; "I'm not going with you. I'm staying with Rosa." "No," screamed Rosa and ran into the house with an

3. **flanks**: the side of the horse between the ribs and back leg
4. **harness**: straps used to attach a horse to wagon
5. **groom**: a horse caretaker

accurate premonition[6] of the inevitability[7] of her fate. I heard the door chain rattle as she set it in place. I heard the lock click. I saw how in addition she ran down the corridor and through the rooms putting out all the lights in order to make herself impossible to find. "You're coming with me," I said to the groom, "or I'll give up the journey, no matter how urgent it is. It's not my intention to give you the girl as the price of the trip." "Giddy up," he said and clapped his hands. The carriage was torn away, like a piece of wood in a current. I still heard the door of my house breaking down and splitting apart under the groom's onslaught, and then my eyes and ears were filled with a roaring sound which overwhelmed all my senses at once. But only for a moment. Then I was already there, as if the farm yard of my invalid[8] opened up immediately in front of my courtyard gate. The horses stood quietly. The snowfall had stopped, moonlight all around. The sick man's parents rushed out of the house, his sister behind them. They almost lifted me out of the carriage. I got nothing from their confused talking. In the sick room one could hardly breathe the air. The neglected cooking stove was smoking. I wanted to push open the window, but first I had to look at the sick man. Thin, without fever, not cold, not warm, with empty eyes, without a shirt, the young man under the stuffed quilt heaved himself up, hung around my throat, and whispered in my ear: "Doctor, let me die." I looked around. No one had heard. The parents stood silently, leaning forward, and waited for my opinion. The sister brought a stool for my handbag. I opened the

---

6. **premonition**: a feeling of stress over a future event
7. **inevitability**: certainty
8. **invalid**: a handicapped person; a person who cannot walk (considered derogative these days)

bag and looked among my instruments. The young man constantly groped at me from the bed to remind me of his request. I took some tweezers, tested them in the candle light, and put them back. "Yes," I thought blasphemously,[9] "in such cases the gods do help. They send the missing horse, even add a second one because it's urgent, and even throw in a groom as a bonus." Now for the first time I thought once more of Rosa. What was I doing? How could I save her? How could I pull her out from under this groom ten miles away with uncontrollable horses in the front of my carriage? These horses, which had somehow loosened their straps, were pushing open the window from outside; I didn't know how. Each one was sticking its head through a window and, unmoved by the crying of the family, observed the invalid. "I'll go back right away," I thought, as if the horses were ordering me to journey back, but I allowed the sister, who thought I was in a daze because of the heat, to take off my fur coat. A glass of rum was prepared for me. The old man clapped me on the shoulder; the sacrifice of his treasure justified this familiarity. I shook my head. In the narrow circle of the old man's thinking I was not well; that was the only reason I refused to drink. The mother stood by the bed and enticed me over. I followed and, as a horse neighed loudly at the ceiling, laid my head on the young man's chest, which trembled under my wet beard. That confirmed what I knew: the young man was healthy. His circulation was a little off, saturated with coffee by his caring mother, but he was healthy and it was best if pushed out of bed with a shove. I was no improver of the world so I let him lie. I was employed by the district and did my duty to the full, right to the point where it was almost too much. Badly paid, but I

---

9. **blasphemously**: speaking out hatefully against god or anything sacred

was generous and ready to help the poor. I still had to look after Rosa, and then the young man might have his way, and I wanted to die too. What was I doing here in this endless winter! My horse was dead, and there was no one in the village who would lend me his. I had to drag my team out of the pigsty. If they hadn't happened to be horses, I'd have had to travel with pigs. That's the way it was. And I nodded to the family. They knew nothing about it, and if they did know, they wouldn't have believed it. Incidentally, it was easy to write prescriptions, but difficult to come to an understanding with people. Now, at this point, my visit might have come to an end—they had once more called for my help unnecessarily. I was used to that. With the help of my night bell the entire region tormented me, but that this time I had to sacrifice Rosa as well, this beautiful girl, who lived in my house all year long and whom I scarcely noticed—this sacrifice was too great, and I had to somehow in my own head subtly rationalize it away for the moment, in order not to let loose at this family who could not, even with their best will, give me Rosa back again. But as I was closing up my handbag and calling for my fur coat, the family stood together, the father sniffing the glass of rum in his hand, the mother, probably disappointed in me—what more do these people expect?—tearfully biting her lips, and the sister flapping a very bloody hand towel. I was somehow ready, in the circumstances, to concede that the young man was perhaps nonetheless sick. I went to him. He smiled up at me, as if I was bringing him the most nourishing kind of soup—ah, now both horses were whinnying, the noise was ordained by heaven to assist my examination of the patient—and now I found out that, yes indeed, the young man was ill. On his right side, in the region of the hip, a wound the size of the palm of one's hand had opened up. Rose colored, in many different shadings, dark in the depths, brighter on the edges, delicately grained, with uneven patches of blood, opened to the light like a mine. That was what it looked like from a distance. Close up, a complication was apparent. Who could look at that without whistling softly? Worms, as thick and long as my little finger, themselves rose colored and also spattered with blood, were wriggling their white bodies with many limbs from their stronghold in the inner of the wound towards the light. Poor young man; there was no helping you. I had found your great wound. You were dying from this flower in your side. The family was happy; they saw me doing something. The sister said that to the mother, the mother told the father, and the father told a few guests who were coming in on tip toe through the moonlight of the open door, balancing themselves with outstretched arms. "Will you save me?" whispered the young man, sobbing, quite blinded by the life inside his wound. That's how people are in my region. Always demanding the impossible from the doctor. They have lost the old faith. The priest sits at home and tears his vestments[10] to pieces, one after the other. But the doctor is supposed to achieve everything with his delicate surgeon's hand. Well, it's what they like to think. I have not offered myself. If they use me for sacred purposes, I let that happen to me as well. What more do I want, an old country doctor, robbed of my servant girl! And so they came, the families and the village elders, and took my clothes off. A choir of school children with the teacher at the head stood in front of the house and sang an extremely simple melody with the words

10. **vestments**: religious robes

Take his clothes off, then he'll heal us,
And if he doesn't cure, then kill him.
It's only a doctor; it's only a doctor.

Then I am stripped of my clothes and, with my fingers in my beard and my head tilted to one side, I looked at the people quietly. I was completely calm and clear about everything and stayed that way, too, although it was not helping me at all, for they were now taking me by the head and feet and dragged me into bed. They laid me against the wall on the side of the wound. Then they all went out of the room; the door was shut; the singing stopped; clouds moved in front of the moon; the bedclothes lay warmly around me; in the open space of the windows the horses' heads swayed like shadows. "Do you know," I heard someone say in my ear, "my confidence in you is very small. You were shaken out from somewhere. You don't come on your own feet. Instead of helping, you give me less room on my deathbed. The best thing would be if I scratched your eyes out." "Right," I said, "it's a disgrace. But now I'm a doctor. What am I supposed to do? Believe me; things are not easy for me either." "Should I be satisfied with this excuse? Alas, I'll probably have to be. I always have to make do. I came into the world with a beautiful wound; that was all I was furnished with." "Young friend," I said, "your mistake is that you have no perspective. I've already been in all the sick rooms, far and wide, and I tell you your wound is not so bad. Made in a tight corner with two blows from an axe. Many people offer their side and hardly hear the axe in the forest, to say nothing of the fact that it's coming closer to them." "Is that really so, or are you deceiving me in my fever?" "It is truly so. Take the word of honor of a medical doctor." He took my word and grew still. But now it was time to think about my escape. The horses were still standing loyally in place. Clothes, fur coat, and bag were quickly snatched up. I didn't want to delay by getting dressed; if the horses rushed as they had on the journey out, I should, in fact, be springing out of that bed into my own, as it were. One horse obediently pulled back from the window. I threw the bundle into the carriage. The fur coat flew too far and was caught on a hook by only one sleeve. Good enough. I swung myself up onto the horse. With the reins dragging loosely, one horse barely harnessed[11] to the other, the carriage swaying behind, last of all in the snow the fur coat. "Giddy up," I said, but there was no giddying up about it. We dragged through the snowy desert like old men; for a long time the fresh but inaccurate singing of the children resounded behind us:

> Enjoy yourselves, you patients.
> The doctor's laid in bed with you.

I'll never come home at this rate. My flourishing practice is lost. A successor is robbing me, but to no avail, for he cannot replace me. In my house the disgusting groom is wreaking havoc.[12] Rosa is his victim. I will not think it through. Naked, abandoned to the frost of this unhappy age, with an earthly carriage and unearthly horses, I drive around by myself, an old man. My fur coat hangs behind the wagon, but I cannot reach it, and no one from the nimble rabble[13] of patients lifts a finger. Betrayed!

---

11. **harnessed**: tied to a wagon
12. **havoc**: devastate (rape)
13. **nimble rabble**: scattered mob

Betrayed! Once one responds to a false alarm on the night bell, there's no making it good again—not ever.

Commentary

Kafka stories have a sense of the fantastic running through them. They are like reading a dream and are often as fragmented as such. Nonetheless, what makes Kafka stories intriguing are that they offer a fresh take on an old format, namely fairy tales. Fairy tales often have heroes go off on a quest for treasure or to rescue a maiden in distress. The heroes also encounter a set of obstacles on the way through which they may test their mettle and become truly heroic. Theseus, for example, sets off to rescue Ariadne from the clutches of the Minotaur. He must overcome the obstacles of the labyrinth and the Minotaur. When he reaches the center of the maze and defeats his nemesis, he emerges victorious with the prize of his princess. Kafka stories, on the other hand, are the opposite of these timeless tales. Kafka crafts "anti-fairy tales" where the heroes set off on their quests yet fail to overcome the obstacles laid before them. More often than not, they fail to achieve their goals and become overwhelmed by both extrinsic and intrinsic forces acting against them. They eventually fall into desperation and are overcome by angst.

The anti-hero's journey begins in "The Country Doctor" with a call for the protagonist doctor to visit a sick man ten miles away. Already there are several obstacles to overcome: a snowstorm and his horse dying the previous night. Heroic journeys usually start off peacefully in idyllic worlds with a wise guide of some sort, guiding the hero from peace into conflict and offering a talisman of some sort to aid in the quest. Journeys of anti-heroes are the opposite: they go from uncomfortable settings and conflict and are lead into absurdity and incongruity. Instead of having the ability to leap into the foray and start his journey, the anti-hero "stood there useless, increasingly covered with snow, becoming all the time more immobile" He fails to even start a successful journey let alone a competent one. There is no aid from a wise guide, no magical talisman. In fact, not one person will lend him a horse. Instead, the antithesis of a wise guide, the immoral groom, offers guidance and magical horses, that appear out of nowhere, as the horses turned from mice to aid Cinderella, not to aid the anti-hero to his goal or to even accomplish it, but to get rid of the anti-hero altogether, so the groom can have his way with the servant girl.

With the first obstacle overcome, albeit one he exercised no free will over, he reaches his destination almost instantaneously. He has descended into the metaphorical underworld. All heroes must enter the belly of the beast to be tried as true heroes, and only with their return can their quest be fulfilled. For Theseus, he entered the labyrinth a man, and he exited a hero. The anti-hero also enters an underworld; conversely, this underworld is one of stagnation and banality. There is no adventure to be had here. From the moment the anti-hero arrives at the invalid's farm, he has lost all control of his life. He no longer has the ability to act for himself. The family members carry him into the house. When he sees his sick patient, he realizes that his goal is futile; the patient does not wish to be healed; instead, he pleads for death. It is at this point, the anti-hero already realizes he has failed. It is not the invalid he was to save, but Rosa, and she is already at the mercy of the hedonistic groom.

As Theseus defeats the Minotaur and gains the love of a princess, the anti-hero is defeated by his goal and loses his princess or prize. The doctor decides to return to rescue his servant girl, but the family obstructs him from leaving. The magical horses, seeming to know more about the state of the patient than the doctor does, draw his attention to the actual sickness. The doctor finally listens and discovers the large wound on the invalid's right side. It is at this moment that the patient changes his desire in accordance to the doctor's. Before, the patient wished for death, now he pleads to be saved. The anti-hero has a chance to be heroic and save the patient when he realizes that saving the servant girl is now too late. Again, he is frustrated from his goal.

The patient's wound is such that he is going to die, being filled with maggots and such. The most the doctor can do is clean the wound and hope it does not get infected. Instead, the family strips the doctor of his clothes. Here, the anti-heroic doctor becomes somewhat of a Christ figure. In the patient's wound, the reader is reminded of Christ's spear wound received on the cross. The children's song reminds the reader further: "Take his clothes off, then he'll heal us,/ And if he doesn't cure, then kill him." When Christ failed to do as expected, his own people had him killed. Many called Christ the God that failed. To non-Christians, Christ is an anti-hero. The doctor is then carried to the patient's bed and laid next to him, similar to Christ being laid in his tomb. What follows is reminiscent of death. "Then they all went out of the room; the door was shut; the singing stopped; clouds moved in front of the moon; the bedclothes lay warmly around me; in the open space of the windows the horses' heads swayed like shadows." A hero suffers death and is raised to the status of a god or suffers to the point of death only to be transformed into a new, better person after. The anti-heroic doctor just takes up the space of the dying patient and can only offer words of comfort.

Seeing the futility of this entire night, the doctor wishes to return home. His final goal is a simple one, and one that he fails at as well. He grabs his clothes and jumps on the sleigh to escape, though he is still naked. The horses fail in magically transporting him safely home, but wander aimlessly in the snowy desert. He is left abandoned by those he wishes to aid, naked, alone, and without hope. If the aim of the hero is to achieve apotheosis and become god or godlike in the annals of time, the anti-hero only achieves alienation, where he is forgotten or "betrayed" to fade away into obscurity.

APPENDIX 1

Study Questions

The Gift of the Magi

1. The power of 3 is a potent symbol in this story. For example, there are 3 gifts of the magi, 3 gifts of the Youngs (gold chain, combs, and love), 3 characters (Jim, Della, and Madame Sofronie), and so on. Find other symbols of three in metaphors, words, and ideas. What does 3 symbolize and why would O. Henry use it throughout this story.

2. O. Henry relishes in paradox. Della and Jim are poverty stricken, yet they are rich in their own love for each other. O. Henry also implements irony in his stories. How is irony used in this story?

3. What does Jim's middle name, Dillingham, seem to represent? Use details from the story to support your answer.

4. What is O. Henry trying to tell us when he sets up the Youngs as having little money but wishing to buy expensive presents? Is giving gifts beyond our means as prevailing as it is in this story? Can you give any examples where you have given beyond your means? If so, why did you do it? Is this a good or bad thing?

5. Is O. Henry being critical of the Youngs in his assessment of their gift-giving? Explain your answer with evidence from the text.

6. A *denouement* is a literary term that means the final "unknotting"

of the plot. A good story has complications, or a "set up", that can only lead to a satisfactory "pay off." What is the *denouement* of this story? You will need to explain what the complication of the story is, and how the denouement resolves the complication.

7. O. Henry asserts that Jim and Della are the "magi" of this story. How is this possible? Explain how symbolism is used to transform Jim and Della of a derelict New York apartment back to the magi of the East who visit the Christ child.

8. Despite an economical writing style, O. Henry is adept at filling his writing with wonderful images. For example, in the fifth paragraph, O. Henry writes, "She stood by the window and looked out dully at a grey cat walking a grey fence in a grey backyard." Write about the meaning of the preceding paragraph and find others of similar potency to comment upon.

9. Word choice plays an important role in understanding story and the author's intent. Consider this from the last part of the story, "And here I have lamely related to you the uneventful chronicle of two foolish children in a flat who most unwisely sacrificed for each other the greatest treasures of their house. But in a last word to the wise of these days let it be said that of all who give gifts these two were the wisest." Why does O. Henry refer to the two protagonists as children? Why would he say "unwisely sacrificed"? Who are "the wise of these days?" If the two "unwisely sacrificed" how are they "the wisest"?

A Respectable Woman

1. What do you think Mrs. Baroda will do when Gouvernail returns next summer? What does she mean when she says she will be nice to him this time? Speculate on what will happen or write your own story depicting what will become of this love triangle.

2. Is Mr. Baroda deserving of what Mrs. Baroda plans on doing? Is it his fault that Mrs. Baroda does not feel passion for him? Who shows more passion in the story, Mr. or Mrs. Baroda? Use evidence from the text to support your answers.

3. Has Mrs. Baroda acted like a respectable woman throughout the story? Could you argue that she, in fact, has not been respectable? Why or why not?

4. Why is the story written in mostly passive voice with a hidden third person narrator? Why is there this secondary narrator? Do you think the narrator was present during the incidents accounted or is the narrator telling a second-hand tale?

5. Is Kate Chopin the actual narrator or is the narrator supposed to be someone else? If someone else then who? If the narrator is Chopin, what can we read into the story? Is the story biased toward Mrs. Baroda?

6. What is your opinion of Gouvernail? Do you think he was trying to seduce Mrs. Baroda or is he completely innocent in this poor woman's "fall"?

7. Is this story a good example of feminism? Why or why not? Use details from the story to support your answer.

Dr. Heidegger's Experiment

1. What is the lesson the doctor has learned by observing the elderly acquaintances behavior?

2. What was the nature of the experiment?

3. Why did the four fail to learn a lesson?

4. What stereotype does each person emulate?

5. If the four elderly friends have a vice, what is Dr. Heidegger's vice? Does he too fail to learn something about himself? Or did he learn all there was through this experiment?

6. Do you think this experiment is ethical? Why or why not? Use examples from the text to support your answer.

7. Edgar Allan Poe criticized Hawthorne's use of allegory as a "heresy" of American fiction. "Dr. Heidegger's Experiment" was one such story criticized. In what ways does the allegory detract from the overall story? Give specific reasons and examples to support the answer.

8. In what ways can the allegory work? Write a summary of the story's allegory only.

An Occurrence at Owl Creek Bridge

1. Ambrose Bierce's writing style has often been compared to Edgar Allan Poe's (though Bierce chaffed at the thought). Compare and contrast the methods Bierce and Poe used to write the two stories supplied in this book.

2. How realistic is this story? How does Bierce use both sight and sound to bring his story into another dimension of imagery?

3. Is Farquhar a sympathetic protagonist? Why or why not? Is he believable as a character? In other words is he well rounded or flat?

4. At what point in the story do you actually realize that Farquhar is delusional (The big reveal in the last sentence of the story does not count)? Where do you realize that he has actually died? Use examples from the story to support your answer.

5. Do you agree with the Federal forces hanging Farquhar without a trial? Does the crime of sabotage warrant capital punishment? Why or why not? Is this type of action still permissible in today's conduct of war? Why or why not?

6. "The wood on either side was full of singular noises, among which–once, twice, and again–he distinctly heard whispers in an unknown tongue." Now that you know that Farquhar is dead in chapter 3, what do the voices symbolize on his walk home? Think about his occupation as a slave owner to help you think about this.

7. "He sees a flutter of female garments; his wife, looking fresh and cool and sweet." Since the Federal forces were notorious for burning plantations, do you think Farquhar's wife has been killed or has she survived? Use examples from the story to support your

answer.

8. Would you consider this an anti-war story? Why or why not? Use examples from the story to support your answer.

9. Read the two poems in Appendix 2 on war. Walt Whitman's poem is about the American Civil War, and Lord Tennyson's poem is about the Crimean War (1854). How is Bierce's short story different in tone and context than these poems? Use examples from both short story and poems to support your answer.

The Tell-Tale Heart

1. Many would assume the narrator is a man. Is there any evidence that the narrator is a woman? Explain.

2. Does Poe create any sympathy for the narrator or are we supposed to only be appalled by his actions?

3. Does the narrator ever show any signs of remorse or is he just a sociopath?

4. This story was very dark and horrifying at the time of publication (1843). Does the story still horrify or disturb you in any way? Why or why not?

5. Poe was never considered a man of literary taste by his contemporaries. Does this story have any literary merit, or is it just a piece of "pulp fiction"? Explain your answer.

6. Which do you find more horrific, the murder the narrator has committed, or the fact that he fails to realize his own madness? Explain your answer with examples from the text.

7. Watch the superb animation of *The Tell-Tale Heart* by Columbia Pictures on the Internet or YouTube (http://kr.youtube.com/watch?v=W4s9V8aQu4c). Does the short animation do the story justice? Did it help add a more visual sense of dread to the story or did it ultimately detract from the reading?

8. Write a response comparing the film and the text.

The Sphinx without a Secret

1. "The Sphinx without a Secret" is ironic in nature. How is irony employed in the text? Use examples from the text to support your answer.

2. What does Oscar Wilde's opinion of women appear to be in this story? Is he positive or negative toward women? Use examples from the text to support your answer.

3. Oscar Wilde is known for his social commentary. What is he saying about Victorian society?

4. Why does Oscar Wilde use the imagery of the sphinx?

5. Why does the story end with Lord Murchison saying, "I wonder"? What is the significance of him saying this phrase at the end of the story?

6. Do you believe the narrator's explanation? Is there an alternative explanation that fits into the scope of the story? If so, what is it?

7. Can the narrator be trusted? Do you think the narrator is actually Oscar Wilde, or is he (or she?) some other personality?

8. If the Lord Murchison loved Lady Alroy so much why did he reject her? Is this perhaps a commentary on how men react towards women more than on how women behave? Does Lord Murchison even give Lady Alroy a chance to explain her mystery? Why not?

9. Many critics and readers feel that a sphinx is supposed to have a secret. What is the secret a sphinx is supposed to have? In most

myths a sphinx has a riddle. What is Wilde really trying to tell the reader when he says a woman is a sphinx without a riddle?

The Open Window

1. A story must have a protagonist and an antagonist. Who is the protagonist of this story? Why?

2. Who is the antagonist in this story? Why?

3. Who the most interesting and least interesting person is in the story? Why?

4. Is the most interesting person the protagonist or antagonist? Is the least interesting the protagonist and antagonist? Why? What is Saki trying to say with these types of characters?

5. Do you know anybody who is like the little girl? How so? How about Mr. Nuttel?

6. What kind of quality to you think the girl has?

7. What is the difference between telling stories that Saki tells and the stories that the girl tells? Is there a difference? Why or why not?

8. Can fiction, or even news reporting, have the same effect on others as the girl's lies have on Mr. Nuttel and Mrs. Sappleton?

9. What influence do stories (fiction or non-fiction) hold over our judgments? Do you think it is important to at least realize that stories of any kind influence our behavior? Why or why not?

A Painful Case

1. Do you consider Mr. Duffy to be a misanthrope? Use examples and details from the story to support your answer.

2. Do you feel that Mr. Duffy was the cause of Mrs. Sinico committing suicide? Why or why not? Use examples and details from the story to support your answer.

3. Why did Captain Sinico allow his wife to meet with Mr. Duffy? Do you think Mr. Duffy is entirely to blame for her suicide? Was Mr. Duffy acting appropriately with another man's wife? Can we totally blame him for how he treated her? Write a response on these ideas. Support your response with examples from the text.

4. When does Mr. Duffy finally realize he is alone? At the end of the story, it tells us he is lonely. But at what other times does he feel his loneliness? Find clues in the text of Mr. Duffy's overwhelming loneliness.

5. The story is written in third person limited point of view, which means that we can only see the story through the protagonist's point of view. However, we get a lot of information about Mrs. Sinico's feelings. Through what technique do we see Mrs. Sinico's point of view without breaking the third person limited point of view?

6. The colors of yellow and brown represent decay in this story. Find examples of Joyce using these colors in his descriptions of people and things and explain how the idea of decay plays into these descriptions.

7. Is there anything heroic about the protagonist? What is or isn't heroic about him?

8. Do you associate with the protagonist at all? Or is he strictly disposable without any redeeming qualities. Explain your answer and support it with examples from the text.

9. How do you personally respond to this story? Do you like it or not? Why or why not? Give your own personal response to the text.

The Mark on the Wall

1. The story begins and ends with the mark on the wall. However, what is the main idea of the story?

2. Some would call this story an essay. Others a short story. What do you think? Support your opinion with evidence from the text.

3. What does the narrator say created the mark on the wall? Make a list of the causes of these marks. What do they have in common? What is Woolf trying to tell the reader by this?

4. At the end of the story, the narrator says, "Ah, the mark on the wall! It was a snail." Why does the narrator say this? Do you think it really could be a snail? Why or why not?

5. Do we, as the narrator, have to trust what the husband says? Why or why not?

6. What does this story say about the difference between how the narrator comes to the conclusion of the mark on the wall and her husband? Is there perhaps a feminist commentary on male and female deduction?

7. Try to write about the mark on the wall with stream of consciousness. Start off thinking about it being some particular, such as a nail. Then write about your thoughts and feelings and have your thoughts flow into other related thoughts.

The Remarkable Case of Davidson's Eyes

1. H.G. Wells deftly combines well known areas of study into his fiction to create verisimilitude, the appearance of the truth. What effect does verisimilitude have on science fiction, especially improbable science fiction? Explain your answer in detail.

2. Compare "Davidson's Eyes" with Bierce's "Owl Creek." Both stories deal with experiencing time out of normal world view. In your opinion, which story is better? Why? Write a comparison/contrast paper on these two stories, highlighting details.

3. At what point in the story do you realize that Davidson's sight perception exists at another place? Use details from the story to support your answer.

4. The story is related in first person through the point of view of Bellows, a secondary character. He never sees any of the events in the story first hand. He relates to the reader only what he has heard. What purpose does such a disconnected narrator serve the overall story?

5. In what ways is such a narrator effective in telling such a story? In what ways is it ineffective?

6. If the narrator has only heard this story from scattered accounts and then retells it to the reader, can the narrator be trusted with retelling an accurate story? Can you trust this narrator? Why or why not? Give examples from the story to support your answer.

7. Why not have Davidson narrate the story? How would the story change in this case?

8. Reread the first paragraph. How would life change if the experiments conducted in this story actually came to pass? How would intercommunication change with the discovery of this type of technology? How about "being watched in our most secret operations by unsuspected eyes"?

9. Write a narrative "of spending an intercalary five minutes on the other side of the world." Where would you go and why would you want to go in this way? In other words, you cannot go in bodily form, but only your sense of vision.

The Diamond Necklace

1. After all Mathilde has suffered through, do you think she is redeemed by the revelation at the end of the story, making this a happy ending? Or is she to continue on in poverty with the knowledge that she has foolishly condemned her family to this state, making this a tragic ending?

2. Will Madame Forestier return to real necklace for compensation over the lost fake one?

3. If Madame Forestier does give the necklace back, will Mathilde have really learned her lesson and save the money, or will she spend it all on what she wants, like she would have at the beginning of the story?

4. What would you have done in the same situation at the end of the story if you were Madame Forestier?

5. What is your opinion of Mathilde? What kind of person is she?

6. What defines the true character of Mathilde: honesty, humility, and hard work or the clothes and jewels that she seeks to cover herself with?

7. If you understand how women were treated in the nineteenth century, can you really blame Mathilde for her actions? What other options would she have to fulfill her sense of self-worth as a woman in a male society?

8. What is your opinion of Loisel? What kind of person is he?

9. Is Mathilde an unfortunate victim of fate (determinism), or is she a victim of her own bad choices that she has made (free-will)? Use the text to support your answer.

10. The men at the ball treated Mathilde as a princess. How would they have treated her if they knew her necklace was a fake?

The Country Doctor

1. Is this story a realistic story? Why or why not? How far into the story can you tell? When do you know?

2. Kafka was known to be afraid of having serious relationships with women. He often visited prostitutes, but found intimate sex revolting, which is why he was always afraid of getting married. Knowing this, what role does Rosa play in the story? How about the groom?

3. Why does the doctor first say the patient is quite healthy and then says he is in serious condition with the wound in his side? What is the significance of this?

4. The story is full of symbolism. What do you think the symbolism is behind each of these characters or ideas? The doctor; the patient; the horses; the wound in the patient's side; the snow; the pigsty; the patient's family; the groom; Rosa.

5. Why does the doctor feel betrayed? Who has betrayed him? Why do you think this person (people) would betray him? Or is his feeling of betrayal only in his mind? If so, explain why he would feel this way?

6. What is the parallel between the country doctor and Kafka the writer? How might they be performing the same function? How does the doctor's anxiety and lack of control translate into Kafka's life? HINT: the doctor often hesitates in his duty and is actually rather useless. Does this have anything to say about Kafka himself? How?

7. Allegory is a type of metaphor (symbol) that extends throughout

the whole story and has meaning separate from the story itself. "The Country Doctor" could be read allegorically. In what ways can the allegory work? Write a summary of the story's allegory only.

8. In what ways does allegory not work? Give specific reasons and examples to support the answer.

APPENDIX 2

War Poetry

Walt Whitman

Cavalry Crossing a Ford

A line in long array where they wind betwixt[1] green islands,
They take a serpentine course, their arms flash in the sun—hark
to the musical clank,
Behold the silvery river, in it the splashing horses loitering[2] stop
to drink,
Behold the brown-faced men, each group, each person a picture,
the negligent[3] rest on the saddles,
Some emerge on the opposite bank, others are just entering the
ford[4]—while,
Scarlet and blue and snowy white,
The guidon[5] flags flutter gaily in the wind.

1. **betwixt**: between
2. **loitering**: waiting around idly
3. **negligent**: careless
4. **ford**: a place where the water is shallow enough to cross
5. **guidon**: a small military flag that identifies a unit

Alfred, Lord Tennyson

The Charge of the Light Brigade

Half a league half a league,
Half a league onward,
All in the valley of Death
Rode the six hundred:
"Forward, the Light Brigade![1]
Charge for the guns" he said:
Into the valley of Death
Rode the six hundred.

"Forward, the Light Brigade!"
Was there a man dismayed?
Not tho'[2] the soldier knew
Some one had blundered:
Theirs not to make reply,
Theirs not to reason why,
Theirs but to do & die,
Into the valley of Death
Rode the six hundred.

Cannon to right of them,
Cannon to left of them,
Cannon in front of them
Volleyed & thundered;
Stormed at with shot and shell,

---

1. **Light Brigade**: the British Light Brigade fought in the Crimean War (1854) against Russia.
2. **tho'**: though (poetic form)

Boldly they rode and well,
Into the jaws of Death,
Into the mouth of Hell
Rode the six hundred.

Flashed all their sabers[3] bare,
Flashed as they turned in air
Sabering the gunners there,
Charging an army while
All the world wondered:
Plunged in the battery[4]-smoke
Right thro' the line they broke;
Cossack[5] & Russian
Reeled from the saber-stroke,
Shattered & sundered.
Then they rode back, but not
Not the six hundred.

Cannon to right of them,
Cannon to left of them,
Cannon behind them
Volleyed and thundered;
Stormed at with shot and shell,
While horse & hero fell,
They that had fought so well
Came thro' the jaws of Death,
Back from the mouth of Hell,

---

3. **saber**: a slightly curved sword used by cavalry
4. **batter**: a combined group of artillery, like cannons
5. **Cossack**: a southern Russian horsemen

All that was left of them,
Left of six hundred.

When can their glory fade?
O the wild charge they made!
All the world wondered.
Honor the charge they made!
Honor the Light Brigade,
Noble six hundred!

Text Notes

All stories are offered on the public domain since they were published before 1921.

Ambrose Bierce: "An Occurrence at Owl Creek Bridge."

Kate Chopin: "A Respectable Woman," from *The Awakening and Selected Short Stories.*

Nathaniel Hawthorne: "Dr. Heidegger's Experiment," from *Twice Told Tales.*

O. Henry: "The Gift of the Magi," from *The Four Million.*

James Joyce: "A Painful Case," from *Dubliners.*

Franz Kafka: "The Country Doctor." Translated by Ian Johnston of Malaspina University-College, Nanaimo, BC, Canada. Offered kindly on the public domain at http://records.viu.ca/~johnstoi/kafka/countrydoctor.htm

Guy de Maupassant: "The Diamond Necklace," from *Original Short Stories—Volume 4.* Translated by A.E. Henderson (offered kindly in the public domain).

Edgar Allan Poe: "A Tell-Tale Heart," from *The Works of Edgar Allan Poe—Volume 2.*

Saki: "The Open Window," from *Beasts and Superbeasts.*

H.G. Wells: "The Remarkable Case of Davidson's Eyes," from *The Country of the Blind, and Other Stories.*

Oscar Wilde: "The Sphinx without a Secret," from Lord *Arthur Savile's Crime, and Other Stories.*

Virginia Woolf: "The Mark on the Wall," from *Monday or Tuesday.*

Glossary

Allegory

A literary work in which the characters and their situations clearly represent general qualities and types—as, in an animal fable, each animal may represent a type of human personality. Often the characters of allegory represent abstract vices or virtues such as avarice, charity, innocence, or prudery.

Ambiguity

Ambiguity refers to the fact that words can often have several meanings, thus creating uncertainty for the reader.

Archetype

An archetype is a basic model from which copies are made. It can be argued that at the heart of all works of literature are certain simple patterns that embody fundamental human concerns, the primary concern being the place of people in the natural world.

Canon

Originally the term canon applied to the list of books in the Hebrew Bible and New Testament which was accepted by church authorities as genuine and having divine authority. Writings not admitted to the canon are called apocrypha. The Protestant and Catholic churches differ as to which writings are apocryphal.

Character

The people in a novel are referred to as characters. We assess them on the basis of what the author tells us about them and on the basis of what they do and say. This is important: we must avoid loose conjecture about a character and establish everything from the evidence of the text. Another point to remember is that the characters are part of a broader pattern: they are members of a society, and the author's distinctive view of how people relate to society will be reflected in the presentation of every character. Details are not included just for their own sake but relate to the overall pattern of the novel.

Comic novels

Novels primarily intended to make us laugh. Students are sometimes grudging in their praise of comic novels, as they can appear lightweight compared to realistic novels, which present such a substantial picture of life. A common, but misguided approach is to ascribe some social purpose to the writer and then to argue that the comedy makes the social criticism entertaining.

Contradiction

Contradiction occurs where we are faced with two or ore meanings that cannot be reconciled or resolved. To this extent it overlaps with ambiguity, but there are important differences. Critics tend to use ambiguity to demonstrate the richness of the texts being discussed. Contradiction, however, which has become a central term in poststructuralist criticism, points to incoherences or divisions in a text that undermine its apparent stability.

Gothic novels

They concentrate on the more sensational side of romance; they depart from the social world, not to seek an ideal goal, but to explore the irrational passions of the mind.

Irony

Irony is a way of writing in which what is meant is contrary to what the words appear to say. Pope, for example, might praise someone extravagantly in his poetry, but the terms used can be so extravagant that they signal to the reader that the person referred to does not deserve such praise.

Metaphor

A figure of speech in which one thing is described in terms of another. A *simile* is very nearly the same, but, whereas metaphor identifies one thing with another, a simile involves the notion of similarity, using the words 'like' or 'as.'

Narrative structure

Narrative is the organization of a series of events into the form of a story. This is obviously what we have in novels; what is less obvious is how similar the narrative structure is in most novels.

Narrator

The narrator tells the story in a novel. Novels contain simple stories which, in their telling, become complicated. There are two overlapping ways by which the novelist can complicate matters. One is by introducing complications in the content: the inclusion of a mass of details about people, places and events makes the story seem substantial and real. The other way in which the writer can complicate matters is by the way in which he or she chooses to narrate the story: a story can be told in many ways, for every narrator will see things from a different point-of-view.

Paradox

A paradox is a statement that appears to be contradictory or inconsistent with common sense—though it may be quite true.

Pathetic fallacy

It objects to the way in which poets attributed human feelings and actions to natural objects.

Plot

Plot is that framework of incidents, however simple or complex, upon which the narrative or drama is constructed, upon which the narrative or drama is constructed; the events of the depicted struggle, as organized into an artistic unit. The elements of plot are a beginning that presumes further action, a middle that presumes both previous and succeeding action, and an end that requires the preceding events but no succeeding action. The unity of the plot is thus the result of necessary relationship and order among the events, not that they center upon a single character.

Postmodernism

Like many of the 'post' terms of modern critical theory, postmodernism has a number of connected uses. In a literal sense it refers to those works of art that were written after the modernist period of the early twentieth century, and whose style differs, often dramatically, from the previous modern style.

Realism

It is particularly associated with the nineteenth-century novel to refer to the idea that texts appear to represent 'the world' 'as it really is.' It means that they will select from their observations the material suitable for constructing a story that faithfully represents what they have understood. Realistic is the label we apply to those novels that seek to provide a convincing illusion of life as we normally think of it. Readers who are just beginning to study novels often feel most comfortable with realistic novels because they appear relatively straightforward. The realistic novel can seem like a clear window on the world—and as readers we can become fully involved with the characters and events—while non-realistic novels seem to look at the world through a distorting mirror, with the result that we are forced to consider the relationship between the work of art itself and life.

Romance

We use the term 'romance' to describe those novels where the story is more adventurous or more fanciful than in realistic novels. Something grander than the novel's familiar concern with social issues is involved, for 'romance' suggests a search for some truth beyond that which we might encounter in ordinary experience. Both characters and events are removed from the everyday, so that there is always an air of the extraordinary about romance.

Satire

The humorous presentation of human folly or vice in such a way as to make it look ridiculous. The satirist aims to correct, by an exposure to ridicule, deviations from normal conduct or reasonable opinion. The chief tool of satire is to exaggerate deformities to the point at which their absurdity is unmistakably apparent.

Science fiction (Sci-Fi)

The informing impulse can be to present a world where the problems for ordinary life are transcended and where the characters can live a more heroic or more ordered life, and ideas that are relevant today may be explored through metaphor to showcase the dramatic direction current thought is leading the world.

Stream of consciousness Technique

A technique which seeks to record the random flow of impressions through a character's mind without any concern for form or convention.

Structure

The structure of a text is its overall shape and pattern. This is sometimes referred to as its form, though strictly speaking form is a more inclusive term which embraces every aspect of the work's technique.

Style

Style means the writer's characteristic manner of expression. What in the end distinguishes one writer from another—so that the experienced reader could identify a passage as coming from, say, a Lawrence novel—is the style. Style change from age to age, but every novelist has his or her own 'voice.'

Utopian novel

They present a perfectly ordered society where all the problems of the real world have been eliminated. This is, however, more than simple day-dreaming: often the intention is that this should reflect back on the imperfections of the existing world.

Index

O. Henry: The Gift of the Magi (1906)
Kate Chopin: A Respectable Woman (1897)
Nathaniel Hawthorne: Dr. Heidegger's Experiment (1837)
Ambrose Bierce: An Occurrence at Owl Creek Bridge (1890)
Edgar Allan Poe: The Tell-Tale Heart (1843)

Oscar Wilde: The Sphinx without a Secret (1891)
Saki: The Open Window (1914)
James Joyce: A Painful Case (1914)
Virginia Woolf: The Mark on the Wall (1921)
H.G. Wells: The Remarkable Case of Davidson's Eyes (1895)

Guy de Maupassant (France): The Diamond Necklace (1884)
Franz Kafka (Germany): The Country Doctor (1919)

Oksun Kang 강옥선

부산대학교 박사
동서대학교 영어학과 교수

저 서: 『블레이크와 작은 천국』(동인, 2004), 공저
Reading British Poetry (동인, 2004), 공저
The Close and Holy Darkness: Discovering Western Short Stories (신아사, 2006), 공저
Eternal Spirit of the Chainless Mind: 12 Themes in English Poetry (신아사, 2007), 공저
논 문: 「낭만기 여성시인의 도덕적 감수성 읽기」(2005)
「블레이크의 예언시와 사회의식」(2001)

Steven Reeder 스티븐 리더

캘리포니아 주립대학 석사
동서대학교 전임강사 (International Studies Program)

저 서: *Reading British Poetry* (동인, 2004), 공저
The Close and Holy Darkness: Discovering Western Short Stories (신아사, 2006), 공저
Eternal Spirit of the Chainless Mind: 12 Themes in English Poetry (신아사, 2007), 공저
논 문: "Dracula as a Tragic Hero: The Illumination of Film on a Text" (2006)
"Kicking Against the Pricks: The Vengeful Pursuit of Retribution in Melville's *Moby-Dick*" (2008)
"Morally Chivalrous: Religious Irony in *Sir Gawain and the Green Knight*" (2008)

Exploring English Short Stories

1판 1쇄 찍음 • 2009년 12월 1일
1판 2쇄 펴냄 • 2014년 9월 11일

지은이 • 강옥선 • 스티븐 리더
발행인 • 정 현 걸
발 행 • 신 아 사
인 쇄 • 예지인쇄

출판등록 • 1956년 1월 5일 (제9-52호)
서울특별시 은평구 녹번동 28-36 2F
전화 02.382.6411 • 팩스 02.382.6401
홈페이지 • www.shinasa.co.kr
이메일 • shinasa@chol.com

ISBN 978-89-8396-665-0 (93840)

정가 **12,000** 원